THE SELF URDU TEACHER

THE SELF URDU TEACHER

EDWARD JOHN

GYAN

Published by

GYAN

Gyan Publishing House
5, Ansari Road
Daryaganj, New Delhi-110002
Phone: 011-47034999, 9811692060
E-mail: books@gyanbooks.com

Distribution Network
gyanbooks.com
India, USA, Canada, UK, Australia, France

ISBN : 978-81-212-3041-4 (PB)

2nd Impression 2020

Printed at: Gyan Press, Delhi.

The Self Urdu Teacher
Author: Edward John

CONTENTS

PART II

Page.

PART III

CHAPTER IX.

CHAPTER X.

Page.

PART IV

CHAPTER XI.

Composition—

Letter-writing etc.—

معلّم زبان اُردو

URDU SELF-TAUGHT

Introduction.

In Part I of this book, the letters of the Urdu language, their names and their sounds and Pronunciations, etc., are explained through the medium of Roman and English. Construction of word by combining letters and formation of sentence by combining words together is shown and for primary teaching some lessons are given so that by reading, writing and learning them the student may have knowledge and practice of reading, writing and understanding Urdu. In Part II, Classification of words or Parts of Speech, Inflexion and Derivation of words and important Grammatical Rules and hints are given, because reading and writing, understanding and speaking a language correctly, depends mainly upon understanding the Grammar of the language very well. Part III contains Rules for the formation of sentences and Lessons for Sentence study. Part IV contains Composition—Conversation, Dialogue, Fables and Essay-writing.

With the aid of this book, enough knowledge of the language can be acquired to get on to conversation and to read easy books in Urdu and improve further.

PART I.

CHAPTER I.

The Alphabet.

LESSON I.

Origin of the Urdu Language

The Urdu language is originated by mixing together the Persian and the Hindi languages. Persian was the language of the Mohamedan kings and of their nobles and lords and Hindi that of the Hindu merchants, shop-keepers and bankers, etc. with whom the soldiers, and their servants had to deal with. When the Urdu language began, all the writing work in the Government offices and courts was done in the Persian alphabet, hence the Urdu letters have been taken from Persian. Of course for some new sounds which were not in Persian but were uttered in Hindi, new letters and symbols have been introduced.

[*Note.*—Urdu is written and printed in two characters—Arabic character and Persian character. The Persian character is generally used in writing and printing books by Lithographic process, but Arabic very seldom. Of course Arabic character is sometimes used in printing books by Typographic process. Arabic character is used in this book as it is printed by Typographic process.]

There are 32 letters in Persian language which are all used in Urdu.

They are—

ج	ث	ت	پ	ب	ا
Jím	Se	Te	Pe	Be	Alif
ر	ذ	د	خ	ح (بڑی)	چ
Re	Zál	Dál	Ḳhe	He (baṛí)	Che
ض	ص	ش	س	ژ	ز
Zwád	Swád	Shín	Sín	Zhe	Ze
ق	ف	غ	ع	ظ	ط
Qáf	Fe	G̣ain	'Ain	Zo	To
و	ن	م	ل	گ	ک
Váo	Nún	Mím	Lám	Gáf	Káf
		ي		ہ (چھوٹي)	
		Ye		He (chhoṭí)	

Of these 32 letters the following have been taken from Arabic, therefore they are sometimes called Arabic letters :—

ط	ض	ص	ذ	ح (بڑي)	ث
To	Zwád	Swád	Zál	He (baṛí)	Se
	ق	ع	ظ		
	Qáf	'Ain	Zo		

Four letters, namely—

گ		چ	پ
Gáf	Zhe	Che	Pe

are not Arabic. These are called Persian letters.

The remaining 19 letters are used in Arabic and Persian both.

Leaving aside the 9 Arabic letters there remain only 23 letters, of which the sounds of the following six are not used in Hindi :—

ق	ف	غ	ژ	ز	خ
Qáf	Fe	Ġain	Zhe	Ze	Ḳhe

The remaining 17 are comprised in Persian and Hindi and these can be called the chief letters of Urdu.

There are 14 such sounds in Hindi, equivalent to which there was no letter in Persian, therefore 3 simple letters *i.e.*,

ڑ	ڈ	ٹ
Re	Dál	Te

and 11 compound letters *viz.*,

چھ	جھ	ٹھ	تھ	پھ	بھ
Chha	Jha	Tha	Tha	Pha	Bha
	گھ	کھ	ڑھ	ڈھ	دھ
	Gha	Kha	Rha	Dha	Dha

have been introduced.

Thus there are altogether 46 letters in Urdu. But now-a-days the above 11 Hindi compound letters are not counted as one letter, and therefore not included in the present-day Alphabet of Urdu. Of course

ڑ	ڈ	ٹ
Ṛe	Ḍál	Ṭe

are included. Including these 3 and 4 more, *i.e.*,

ے	ء	لا	ھ
Baṛí ye	Hamza	Lám-alif	Dochashmí he

which are added in the Alphabet, there are 39 letters now-a-days.

LESSON 2.

[*Note.*—Urdu is read and written from right to left.]

Hurúf-i-tahajjì kí Taqsím.

Division of Alphabet.

Urdu letters are divided into (1) Hurúf-i-masmat or Hurúf-i-sahíh **(Consonants)** and (2) Hurúf-i-maswat or Hurúf-i-illat **(Vowels)**.

1. *Harf-i-masmat*—**Consonant.**

Harf-i-masmat or sahíh **Consonant** is that which cannot be sounded without the help of a vowel.

They are as follows :—

The Urdu Alphabet as in force now-a-days.

Harfoṉ ke nám aur sùrat.

Names and Forms of Letters.

(*Arabic character*)

ٹ TE	ت TE	پ PE	ب BE	ALIF
خ ḲHE	ح (بڑی) HE (baṛi)	چ CHE	ج JÍM	ث SE
ڑ ṚE	ر RE	ذ ZÁL	ڈ ḌÁL	د DÁL
ص SWÁD	ش SHÍN	س SÍN	ژ ZHE	ز ZE
غ G̣AIN	ع AIN	ظ ZO	ط TO	ض ZWAD
ل LÁM	گ GÁF	ک KÁF	ق QÁF	ف FE
ھ DOCHASHMI HE	ہ (چھوٹی) HE (chhoṭí)	و VÁO	ن NÚN	م MÍM
ے (بڑی) YE (baṛí)	ی (چھوٹی) YE (chhoṭí)		ء HAMZA	لا LÁM-ALIF

LESSON 3.

Hurúf-i-masmat or sahíh kí áwázen

Sounds of Consonants.

ا Alif—sounds as Roman *a* in 'agar' or English *u* in 'up'.

ب Be—sounds as *b*.

پ Pe—sounds as *p*.

ت Te } —no such sound in English. It sounds as
ط To } soft Roman *t* in 'terá'.

ٹ Ṭe—sounds as English *t* in 'to' or Roman *t* in 'topí'.

ث Se }
س Sín } —sounds as *s*.
ص Swád }

ج Jim—sounds as *j*.

چ Che—sounds as *ch*.

ح (بڑی) }
ھ (دو چشمی) } He—sounds as *h*.
ہ (چھوٹی) }

خ Khe—no such sound in English. It is equivalent to Roman 'kh'.

د Dál—sounds as *th* in 'thus' or Roman *d* in 'das'

ڈ Dal—sounds as *d* in 'do' or Roman *ḍ* in 'ḍol'.

ذ Zál }
ز Ze }
ض Zwád } —sound as *z*.
ظ Zo }

ر Re—sounds as *r*.

ڑ Ṛe—no such sound in English. It is equivalent to Roman *ṛ*.

ژ Zhe—sounds as *s* in 'leisure'.

ش Shín—sounds as *sh*.

ع 'Ain—no such sound in English. It sounds as Roman *a* in ''aql' uttered from the depth of the throat.

غ Ġain—no such sound in English. It sounds like Roman 'g' in 'gul'.

ف Fe—sounds like *f*.

ق Qáf—sounds as *q*.

ک Káf—sounds as *k*.

گ Gáf—sounds as *g* in 'go.'

ل Lám—sounds as *l*.

م Mím—sounds as *m*.

ن Nún—sounds as *n*.

(*Note*—Undotted ں nún called Nún Ġunna gives nasal sound as Roman *n̲* in 'bán̲' or English *n* in 'ant').

و Váo—sounds as *w*, *v*.

لا Lám-alif—sounds as English *la* in 'large'.

ء Hamza—it is marked over و, ی and ے indicating their sounds as او alif váo pesh = *o* or ؤ hamza váo pesh = *o*; ای alif ye zer = *í* or ئی hamza ye zer = *í*; اے alif ye zer = *e* or ئے hamza ye zer = *e*.

(چھوٹی) ی Ye (chhoṭí)—sounds as *ee* in 'bee'.

(بڑی) ے Ye (baṛí)—sounds as *a* in 'take'.

Exercise

Write the forms of letters of the following names in Urdu :—

gáf	te	qáf	alif	pe	dochasmi he
dal	lám	re	mím	ḳhe	ġain
baṛí he	káf	dál	'ain	zál	swád
sín	chhoṭíhe	che	ze	be	chhoṭí ye
ṛe	to	fe	baṛí ye	se	te
zhe	shín	zo	hamza	lám-alif	nun vao

Write the names of the following letters in Roman :—

لا ے ی ک د ڈ ف ۂ ح ھ ظ ط

س غ پ ش ڑ ص خ ا ژ ب ز ع

ر ٹ ن ں ث چ و ل گ ڑ ق م

و ٹ

Write Roman or English letters for the sounds of the following :—

ر ن ث چ د ل گ لا ے ی ک ہ

ف ۂ ح ھ ظ س ش پ ث ٹ ڈ خ

ڑ ق م و ز ژ س

Write Urdu letters for the sounds of the following Roman and English letters :—

r k b s n f ṛ t d ḳh h
a la ch zh ḍ n̲ l g g q ee
sh m p v ṭ j z 'a n̲ ye

Distinguish :—

م ڈ ڑ ر س ح ط و غ ژ ڑ ص
ہ مو خ ت ز ل ف ث گ ک ھ ق
ع ج ڑ ے چ ڈ ی ں ط ص ظ ض
ں ع لا

LESSON 4.

2. *Harf-i-maswat or 'illat*—Vowel.

Hurf-i-maswat or 'illaṭ (**Vowel**) is that which can be sounded by itself.

Hurúf-i-maswat or 'illat (**Vowels**) are of two kinds :—

(1) Maqsúrah (**Short**), (2) Mamdúdah (**Long**).

1. Maswat-i-maqsúrah (**Short vowel**) is that which has a short suppressed sound. They are three—

(1) (َ) Fatah or Zabar
(2) (ِ) Kasra or Zer
(3) (ُ) Zamma or Pesh

These are also called " Harkát " and " 'Airáb "

Vowel points. They are never used alone but are used in uttering forth the Harf-i-masmat (Consonant), as, بَ *ba.* Here the letter ب *b* is consonant but it cannot be sounded unless the sound of zabar is applied to it.

As these Maswat-i-maqsúrah are not used alone people count them as the symbols of sounds and therefore they are not included in the Hurúf-i-tahajjí (Alphabet).

2. Maswat-i-mamdúdah (**Long Vowel**) is that which has a long sound.

They are three :—

ا و ی

The Maswat-i-mamdúdah (Long Vowel) when combined with Harf-i-masmat (Consonants) they prolong their sounds, as by combining ب be and اَ alif zabar = با *bá* ; ب be and وُ váo pesh = بو *bú* ب be and یِ ye zer = بی *bí.*

ا و ي are not always Harf-i-maswat or 'illat (Vowels). They are used as Harf-i-masmat of sahíh (Consonants) also. Then they too need a vowel like consonants.

As they are sometimes Maswat (Vowels) and sometimes Masmat (Consonants) they are called Ním maswat (**Semi-vowels**).

LESSON 5.

Hurúf-i-maswat yá Harkát yá Airáb ki áwázen̲ aur iste'mál.

Use and sounds of Vowel points.

Maswat-i-maqsúrah—Short Vowels.

(َ)Zabar—it sounds as Roman *a* in 'agar' or English *u* in 'up,' when at the beginning of a word, but when combined with other letters, it sounds long as Roman *á* in 'dám' or English *a* in 'part.' It is marked over the letters (consonants), as

اَ alif zabar = a ; بَ be zabar = ba ;

پَ pe zabar = pa, and so on.

(ِ) Zer—it sounds as Roman *i* in 'itná' or English *i* in 'sit.' It is marked under the letters (consonants), as, اِ alif zer = i ; بِ be zer = bi ; پِ pe zer = pi, and so on.

(ُ) pesh—it sounds as Roman *u* in 'utná' or English *oo* in good. It is marked over the letters as اُ alif pesh = u ; بُ be pesh = bu ; پُ pe pesh = pu, and so on.

Maswat-i-mamdúdah yá Nim maswat.

Long Vowels or Semi-vowels.

ا alif—when combined with other letters with mark (َ) zabar over it sounds long as Roman *á* in ' ká ' or English *a* in 'cart,' as, ب be ا alif zabar= با bá ; ح he ا alif zabar = حا há, etc.

و váo—when combined with other letters with (ُ) over it (now-a-days some people use up-set pesh (ٗ) in manuscripts for the long sound of Roman *ú* or English *oo* while others do not) it sounds as Roman *ú* in ' tú ' or English *oo* in ' fool,' as ب be ُو váo pesh = bú پ pe ُو váo pesh = پُو pú, etc. Some people use (ُ) on و for the sound of O as کُو káf váo pesh ' ko ' ,اُو alif váo pesh O while others do not. It remains understood.

ی ye—when combined with other letters with mark (ِ) zer under it, it sounds as Roman *í* in ' pání' or English *ee* in 'see,' as ج jím یِ ye zer = جِي jí ; د dál یِ ye zer = دِي dí, etc.

LESSON 6.

Diacritical marks and Symbols.

Following are some of the diacritical marks and symbols :—

(ً) tanwín
(ّ) tashdíd
(ٓ) madd
(ء) hamza
(ٗ) ulṭá pesh
(ۂ) laṭkan he

Use and sounds of Diacritical marks and symbols.

(ً) tanwín—It is marked over ا alif when it comes last in some words to indicate the sound of *an* مثلاً maslan (for example, as).

(ّ) tashdid—It is marked over letters to indicate its sound double, as امّا ammá (mother, mamma), بچّہ bachcha (infant).

(ٓ) madd—It is marked over ا alif to prolong its sound when comes first in any word, as (ا) alif (ٓ) madd (َ) zabar = آ á like Roman *á* in 'kám' or English *a* in 'part.'

(ء) hamza—It is also a symbol used over 'letters although now-a-days included in the letters. It is marked over و váo and ی ye helping in uttering their peculiar sounds instead of using ا alif for it, as پ pe اَ alif zabar =pá, ئِ hamza ye zer í = پائي pái ; ج jím اَ alif zabar جا já, ؤُ hamza váo pesh o = جاؤ jáo.

(ٗ) ulṭá pesh—Now-a-days it is marked over ‚ generally in manuscripts to indicate its sound long as ا alif ‚ váo pesh =اُو oo, as Roman ú in 'sút' or English *oo* in 'boot.'

(ھ) laṭkan he—This form is used for ہ chhoṭi he in combination, as کہا kahá (said). In manuscript a shosha (particle) like that of ب پ etc. (ـہ) or like laṭkan he is combined to the letters and (ٖ) is marked under it.

Exercise.

(َ) Zabar

جَ ja	ثَ sa	ٹَ ṭa	تَ ta	پَ pa	بَ ba	اَ a
رَ ra	ذَ za	ڈَ ḍa	دَ da	خَ kha	حَ ha	چَ cha
ضَ za	صَ sa	شَ sha	سَ sa	ژَ zha	زَ za	ڑَ ṛa
کَ ka	قَ qa	فَ fa	غَ ag	عَ 'a	ظَ za	طَ ta
يَ ya	ہَ, ھَ ha	وَ va	نَ na	مَ ma	لَ la	گَ ga

(ِ) Zer

جِ ji	ثِ si	ٹِ ṭi	تِ ti	پِ pi	بِ bi	اِ i
رِ ri	ذِ zi	ڈِ ḍi	دِ di	خِ khi	حِ hi	چِ chi
ضِ zi	صِ si	شِ shi	سِ si	ژِ zhi	زِ zi	ڑِ ṛi
کِ ki	قِ qi	فِ fi	غِ gi	عِ 'i	ظِ zi	طِ ti
یِ yi	ہِ ھِ hi	وِ vi	نِ ni	مِ mi	لِ li	گِ gi

(ُ) Pesh

جُ ju	ثُ su	ٹُ ṭu	تُ tu	پُ pu	بُ bu	اُ u
رُ ru	ذُ zu	ڈُ ḍu	دُ du	خُ khu	حُ hu	چُ chu
ضُ zu	صُ su	شُ shu	سُ su	ژُ zhu	زُ zu	ڑُ ṛu
کُ ku	قُ qu	فُ fu	غُ go	عُ 'u	ظُ zu	طُ tu
یُ yu	ہُ ھُ hu	وُ vu	نُ nu	مُ mu	لُ lu	گُ gu

Write Roman equivalents of:—

غِ	چَ	ضُ	ڈَ	ہُ	شَ
ظَ	عَ	ٹَ	گُ	حَ	ھِ طِ

ڑِ　ک　ٹُ　فِ　نَ　قُ　سِ

مُ　ڑِ　لَ　جِ　نُ　ژَ　رِ

پَ　خُ　ذِ　یُ　ٹِ　صَ

Write Urdu equivalents of :—

da	shi	ga	ṛu	qu
zu	fi	si	ra	na
ḍa	ga	mi	ru	'i
ki	hu	hi	ma	vu
zi	pa	nu	mi	ga
ti	hi	'u	fa	la
ji	qa	shu	ṭu	ḳhi
zha	yu	sa	du	pa

LESSON 7.

Harfon ki Miláwaṭ

Combination of Letters

Unki Banáwaṭ, Talaffuz aur Hijje

Their combined Forms, Pronunciations and Spelling

(ا) *ki miláwaṭ*

Combination of (ا)

A

[*Read from left to right*]

اَب zabar ab	اِب zer ib	اُب pesh ub
اَپ „ ap	اِپ „ ip	اُپ „ up

أَت	zabar	at	إِت	zer	it	أُت	pesh	ut
أَٹ	„	aṭ	إِٹ	„	iṭ	أُٹ	„	uṭ
أَث	„	as	إِث	„	is	أُث	„	us
أَج	„	aj	إِج	„	ij	أُج	„	uj
أَچ	„	ach	إِچ	„	ich	أُچ	„	uch
أَح	„	ah	إِح	„	ih	أُح	„	uh
أَخ	„	aḳh	إِخ	„	iḳh	أُخ	„	uḳh
أَد	„	ad	إِد	„	id	أُد	„	ud
أَڈ	„	aḍ	إِڈ	„	iḍ	أُڈ	„	uḍ
أَذ	„	az	إِذ	„	iz	أُذ	„	uz
أَر	„	ar	إِر	„	ir	أُر	„	ur
أَڑ	„	aṛ	إِڑ	„	iṛ	أُڑ	„	uṛ
أَز	„	az	إِز	„	iz	أُز	„	uz
أَژ	„	azh	إِژ	„	izh	أُژ	„	uzh
أَس	„	as	إِس	„	is	أُس	„	us
أَش	„	ash	إِش	„	ish	أُش	„	ush
أَص	„	as	إِص	„	is	أُص	„	us
أَض	„	az	إِض	„	iz	أُض	„	uz
أَط	„	at	إِط	„	it	أُط	„	ut
أَظ	„	az	إِظ	„	iz	أُظ	„	uz

أَع	zabar a'a		إِع	zer i'		أُع	pesh u'
أَغ	,,	ag	إِغ	,,	ig	أُغ	,, ug
أَف	,,	af	إِف	,,	if	أُف	,, uf
أَق	,,	aq	إِق	,,	iq	أُق	,, uq
أَک	,,	ak	إِک	,,	ik	أُک	,, uk
أَگ	,,	ag	إِگ	,,	ig	أُگ	,, ug
أَل	,,	al	إِل	,,	il	أُل	,, ul
أَم	,,	am	إِم	,,	im	أُم	,, um
أَن	,,	an	إِن	,,	in	أُن	,, un
أَو	,,	av	إِو	,,	iv	أُو	,, uv
أَه	,,	ah	إِه	,,	ih	أُه	,, uh
			إِی	,,	i		
أَے	,,	ai	إِے	,,	e		

B

In constructing words instead of original full form of letters their particles (shoshe) are added together.

There are two or three kinds of forms of the particles (shoshe)—beginning, middling and ending.

[*Note.*—Particles (shoshe) of the letters of the same form differing only in dots, strokes and sounds have been repeated such as, for ج چ ح خ (حـ ـحـ ـح).

Shoshe (Particles) of the letters when used in Combination—beginning, middling, and ending.

ا ب......ث ن ي ج......خ س ش ص ض ط ظ

(ا ا) (بـ ـبـ ـب) (حـ ـحـ ـح) (سـ ـسـ ـس) (صـ ـصـ ـص) (ط ط)

ع غ   ف ق   ک گ   ل   م   ہ

(عـ ـعـ ـع) (فـ ـفـ ـق) (کـ ـکـ ـک) (لـ ـلـ ـل) (مـ ـمـ ـم) (ہـ ـہـ ـہ)

Combination of Particles of letters showing their connecting points

شـ ـفـ ـقـ ـت   شـ ـہـ ـر   مـ ـعـ ـلـ ـو ـم   نـ ـقـ ـشـ ـہ

خـ ـو ا ہـ ـش   کـ ـمـ ـبـ ـخـ ـت   مـ ـقـ ـد ـم   شـ ـکـ ـل

چـ ـمـ ـن   شـ ـکـ ـر ـقـ ـنـ ـد   گـ ـفـ ـتـ ـگـ ـو   مـ ـطـ ـلـ ـب

مـ ـلـ ـز ا ـت   چـ ـنـ ـا نـ ـچـ ـہ   سـ ـنـ ـلـ ـج   ہـ ـیـ ـضـ ـہ

چـ ـلـ ـگـ ـل   سـ ـلـ ـیـ ـچـ ـر   مـ ـشـ ـکـ ـو ـر   شـ ـلـ ـجـ ـم

قـ ـو ا ہـ ـد   تـ ـلـ ـد ـر   سـ ـنـ ـی قـ ـلـ ـع   مـ ـنـ ـصـ ـد

ا ـنـ ـگـ ـلـ ـسـ ـتـ ـا ـن مـ ـکـ ـمـ ـو ـد   مـ ـشـ ـکـ ـو ـک   ا ـصـ ـلـ ـیـ ـت

نـ ـبـ ـیـ ـن   قـ ـسـ ـم   فـ ـتـ ـصـ ـمـ ـد   بـ ـغـ ـل

بـ ـغـ ـلـ ـگـ ـیـ ـر   ہـ ـمـ ـا ـلـ ـیـ ـہ   سـ ـلـ ـگـ ـسـ ـا ـر   کـ ـچـ ـیـ ـہ

LESSON 8.

(ب) *kí miláwaṭ*

Combination (ب)

[*Read from left to right*],

بآ bá

بَب bab   بِب bib   بُب bub   بَپ bap   بِپ bip   بُپ bup

بَت bat   بِت bit   بُت but   بَٹ baṭ   بِٹ biṭ   بُٹ buṭ

بَث bas بِث bis بُث bus بَج baj بِج bij بُج buj

بَچ bach بِچ bich بُچ buch بَح bah بِح bih بُح buh

بَخ bakh بِخ bikh بُخ bukh بَد bad بِد bid بُد bud

بَڈ baḍ بِڈ biḍ بُڈ buḍ بَذ baz بِذ biz بُذ buz

بَر bar بِر bir بُر bur بَڑ baṛ بِڑ biṛ بُڑ buṛ

بَز baz بِز biz بُز buz بَژ bazh بِژ bizh بُژ buzh

بَس bas بِس bis بُس bus بَش bash بِش bish بُش bush

بَص bas بِص bis بُص bus بَض baz بِض biz بُض buz

بَط bat بِط bit بُط but بَظ baz بِظ biz بُظ buz

بَع b'a بِع b'i بُع b'u بَغ bag بِغ big بُغ bug

بَف baf بِف bif بُف buf بَق baq بِق biq بُق buq

بَک bak بِک bik بُک buk بَگ bag بِگ big بُگ bug

بَل bal بِل bil بُل bul بَم bam بِم bim بُم bum

بَن ban بِن bin بُن bun بَو bav بِو biv بُو buv

بَہ بَھ bah بِہ بِھ bih بُہ بُھ buh بِی bi

[*Note.*—Combine پ ت ٹ ث ن ی with letters in the same way as ب is combined above. Shoshe (particles) of پ ت ٹ ث ن ي shall be the same as of ب. Difference will be only in sounds and dots.]

LESSON 9.

(ج) *kí miláwaṭ*

Combination (ج)

جا já

جَب jab جِب jib جُب jub جَپ jap جِپ jip جُپ jup

جَت jat جِت jit جُت jut جَٹ jaṭ جِٹ jiṭ جُٹ juṭ

جَث a جِث jis جُث jus جَج jaj جِج jij جُج juj

جَچ jach جِچ jich جُچ juch جَح jah جِح jih جُح juh

جَخ jakh جِخ jikh جُخ jukh

jad جَد jid جِد jud جُد

Add ڈ and ذ to جہ as added د to جہ and put their dots, as جَڈ جَذ etc

جَر jar جِر jir جُر jur

Add ژ ز ذ to جـ as added ر to ج and put their dots جَز جَز جَژ

جَس jas جِس jis جُس jus جَش jash جِش jish جُش jush

جَص jas جِص jis جُص jus جَض jaz جِض jiz جُض juz

جَط jat جِط jit جُط jut جَظ jaz جِظ jiz جُظ juz

جَع j'a جِع j'i جُع j'u جَغ jag جِغ jig جُغ jug

جَف jaf جِف jif جُف juf جَق jaq جِق jiq جُق juq

جَک jak جِک jik جُک juk جَگ jag جِگ jig جُگ jug

جَل jal جِل jil جُل jul جَم jam جِم jim جُم jum

جَن jan جِن jin جُن jun جَو jav جِو jiv جُو juv

جَهه jah جِهه jih جُه juh جِي ji

جه jah جے je

Combine خ ح چ with letters in the same way as جـ.

ژ ز ذ ر ڈ د cannot be joined to any letter at their ends.

LESSON 10

(س ش) *kí miláwaț.*

Combination of (س ش)

[*Note.*—There is only difference of dots between س and ش hence ش not repeated.]

سا sá

سَب sab سِب sib سُب sub سَپ sap سِپ sip سُپ sup

Add ث ٹ ت پ to س as سَب etc.

سَج saj سِج sij سُج suj

Add خ ح چ to س as سَچ etc.

سَد sad سِد sid سُد sud etc.

Add ذ ڈ to س as سَد above.

سَر sar سِر sir سُر sur etc.

Add ژ ڑ ز to س as سَر etc. above.

سَس sas سِس sis سُس sus سَش sash سِش sish سُش sush

سَص sas سِص sis سُص sus—in the same way add ض

سَط sat سِط sit سُط sut—in the same way add ظ

سَع s'a سِع s'i سُع s'u—in the same way add غ

سَف saf etc. سَق saq etc.

سَک sak etc. سَگ sag etc

سَل sal etc. سَم sam etc.

سَن san etc. سَو sav etc.

سَہ سَھ sah etc. سِی sí

سَے sai سے se

.LESSON 11.

No pesh and zer can be used with combined (ا)alif.

Use vowel points zebar, zer pesh with each of the following combined forms and read.

(ص ض) *kí miláwat.*

Combination of (ص ض).

[*Note.*—Difference of only dots between ص and ض].

صاحب....صث صح....صج صد صق صف صر

صز صس صش صص صض صط صظ صع صغ

صف صق صک صگ صل صم صن صو صہ

صھ صا صي صے

(ط ظ) *kí miláwaṭ.*

Combination of (ط ظ).

طا طب.........طث طج......طخ طد طذ طر

طر.........طژ طس طش طص طض طط طظ طع طغ

طف طق طک طگ طل طم طن طو طہ

طھ طی طے

(1) Pesh cannot be used with ے barí ye.

(2) No pesh and zer can be used with combined (ا) alif.

(ع غ) *kí miláwaṭ.*

Combination of (ع غ)

عا عب.........عث عج.........عخ عد عڈ عذ عد

عذ عز.........عژ عس عش عص عض عط عظ

عع عغ عف عق عک عگ عل عم عن عو

عہ عھ عی عے

(ف ق) *kí miláwaṭ.*

Combination of (ف ق).

فا فب.........فث فج.........فخ فد فڈ فذ

فز.........فژ فس فش فص فض فط فظ فع فغ

فف فق فک فل فم فن فو فہ فھ فی فے

(ک گ) *ki miláwaṭ.*

Combination of (ک گ).

کا گا کب گب.........کث کج.........کخ کد کذ

کذ کر......کژ کس کش کص کض کط کظ

کع کغ کف کق کک کگ کل کم کن کو کہ

کھ کی کے

(ل) *kí miláwaṭ.*

Combination of (ل)

لا لب.........لث لج.........لخ لد لڈ لذ لر......لژ

لس لش لص لض لط لظ لع لغ لف لق لک لگ

لل لم لن لو لہ لھ لي لے

(م) *kí miláwaṭ.*

Combination of (م)

ما مب.........مث مج......مخ مد مڈ مذ

مر.........مژ مس مش مص مض مط مظ مع مغ

مف مق مک مگ مل مم من مو مہ مھ

مي مے

(ہ ھ) *kí miláwaṭ.*

Combination of

[*Note.*—This form or (ہ) chhoṭi comes at the end of a word combined or uncombined.]

ھا ھب.........ھث ھج.........ھخ ھد ھڈ ھذ
ھر.........ھژ ھس ھش ھص ھض ھط ھظ ھع
ھغ ھف ھق ھک ھگ ھل ھم ھن ھو ھہ
ھی ھے

CHAPTER II.

LESSON 1.

Kalma yá Lafz—Word

Whatever a man speaks is called a Lafz or Kalma **(Word)**.

Words having some meaning are called Mauzu' (significant) and those having no meaning are called Mohmal (meaningless).

Lafzoṉ ki Banáwaṭ

Formation of Words

Two or more letters added together and having some meaning form a Lafz (Word).

Words of two single letters.

اَب ab—now	اِس is—this
اِن in—these	اُڑ uṛ—fly
اُن un – those	اُس us—he, she, it
دَم dam—breath	دَر dar—door

دِن din—day

دے de—give

رَس ras—sap

زَر zar—gold, riches

رُو rú—face

رُخ rukh—side

دُر dur—pearl

دُو do—two

وہ wuh—he

آڑ áṛ—curtain

آم ám—mango

آہ áh—sigh

آج—to-day

دَہ dah—ten

رَب rab—God

رَگ rag—vein, nerve

زَن zan—woman

رُک ruk—stop

رَہ rah—stay, live

دِل dil—heart

ڈَر ḍar—fear

اَے ae—O!

آپ áp—you, self

آس ás—hope

آگ ág—fire

آب áb—water

[*Note.*—(آ) alif with madd over it is called Alif Mamdúdah].

Exercise

Write Urdu equivalents of :—

is	uṛ	dar	rab	zan	dil
ae	ḍar	wuh	do	dah	rag
in	ras	dur	dam	ab	din

rú un zar rukh de us

ruk rah áṛ ág áj ám

áp áh ás

Write Roman equivalents of :—

رَہ دے رُخ دُو اُن رَس دَہ آگ

آم رُک اِس زَن رَب رُو آے دُر

آس رَگ دِل زَر دَر اَڑ اِن آج

آہ اُس اَب دَم وُہ ڈَر دِن آڑ

آپ

LESSON 2.

Words of three single Letters.

رات rát—night	دال dál—pulse
داب dáb—pressure	داد dád—justice, gift
داغ dág—speck, blemish	دام dám—price
اور aur—and	راج ráj—kingdom
راہ ráh—way	راگ rág—tune
ڈاک ḍák—mail	راب ráb—treacle
دَوڑ dauṛ—race	ڈُول ḍol—bucket
زُور zor—force, stress	دُور dúr—far
زَرد zard—yellow	دَرد dard—pain

ڈال ḍá—branch زاغ zág—crow
ران rán—thigh رال rál—resin, saliva
راے ráe—opinion رائی rái—mustard

[*Note*—When (ا) comes between other letters combined or uncombined zabar is understood and madd is not used.]

Sih horfi lafzon ki hijje ká tariqa

The way of spelling the three lettered words.

There are two ways—

For example :—

(1) رات—ر re alif ت te zabar = رات rát

دور—د dal , váo ر ṛe zabar = دَور daur

ڈول—ڈ ḍál , váo ل lám pesh = ڈُول dol

(2) رات—ر re آ alif zabar را , ت te mauqúf or sákin = رات rát

دور—د dál , váo zabar دَو dau ر ṛe mauqúf or sákin = دور dáuṛ

ڈول—ڈ ḍál , váo pesh ڈو ḍo ل lám mauqúf or sákin = ڈول ḍol

Exercise.

Write Urdu equivalents of :—

dál	dard	rál	ḍol
dám	ráb	rái	rán
dák	aur	dauṛ	ráj

dád	dúr	zard	ráh
zor	rág	ḍál	ráe
rát	dáb	zág	dág

Write Roman equivalents of :—

زور	ڈال	راے	زرد	دور
رات	ڈاک	زاغ	اور	راہ
راب	ڈُول	دَور	رائي	دال
داد	ران	راہ	راج	دام

LESSON 3.

Words of four single letters.

دادا dádá—grandfather

ادرک adrak—ginger

آرام árám—rest

آزاد ázád—free

دَورَہ daurah—tour

وارِد wárid—coming

وَرزِش warzish—exercise

رُوزَہ roza—fast

رُوزي rozí—daily food

وَردي wardí—uniform

دادي dádí—grandmother

آداب ádáb—respects

ڈُورہ ḍorah—thread

وادي wádi—valley

وِداع widá'—farewell

وارا wárá—cheapness

رَوزَن rauzan—hole

وارِث wáris—heir

Chahár harfí lafzoṉ kí hijje ká tariqa.

The way of spelling the four-lettered words.

For example :—

دَادَا—د dál ا alif zabar دَا dá, د dál ا alif zabar dá = دادا dádá.

دَوْرَہ—د dál و váo zabar دَو dau ر re ہ he zabar rah = دوره daurah.

وِدَاع—و zer وِ vi داع dá' zabar داع dá' = وداع widá'.

Exercise.

Write Urdu equivalents of :—

adrak	widá	ádáb	dádí
wárid	wardí	ḍorah	ázád
wádí	rauzan	rozí	wáris
roza	warzish	wárá	dádá
árám	daurah	wardí	

Write Roman equivalents of :—

زَردِی دادی آزاد دَادَا وَردِی

دَورہ آداب ڈورہ رُوزِی وَارَا

رُوزہ آرام وِداع رَوزَن وَرزِش

آدرک وارد وادِی

LESSON 4.

Words of two combined letters.

پَر	par—on	بَس	bas—enough
خَر	khar—ass	هَم	ham—we
تُم	tum—you	هَے	hai—is
پُل	pul—bridge	غَم	gam—sorrow, grief
هَل	hal—plough	حَق	haq=right
هَار	hár—defeat	چُپ	chup—silent
خط	khat—letter	بَط	bat—duck
صَف	saf—row, line	غُل	gul—noise
تَن	tan—body	تَب	tab—then
جَب	jab—when	کَب	kab—when
سَب	sab—all	کُل	kull—whole
کُو	ko—to	کَا-کِي-کے	ká, kí, ke—of
جُو	jo—which, that	پَس	pas—so
لَڑ	lar—fight	کَر	kar—do
لَو	lo—take	مَت	mat—don't

جا já—go	لا lá—bring
سے so—from	بد bad—bad
تک tak—till, to	کم kam—less
لب lab—lip	مس mis—touch
ہو ho—be, are	کہ ki—that
یہ yih—this	وہ wuh—that, he, she, it
تو tú—thou	بو bú—smell

LESSON 5.

Words of three combined letters.

پاس pás—near	تاج táj—crown
ناپ náp—measure	تال tál—tank
آیا áyá—came	گیا gayá—went
ناک nák—nose	نام nám—name
بال bál—hair	باپ báp—father
ہوش hosh—sense	جان ján—life
چار chár—four	بات bát—talk, thing

چائے	cháe—tea	شام	shám—evening
شور	shor—noise	صاف	sáf—clean
سونا	soná—gold	طاق	táq—shelf
شاہ	sháh—king	قسم	qism—kind
مگر	magar—but	مال	mál—property
مور	mor—peacock	تھا	thá—was
کھا	khá—eat	پھر	phir—again
گھر	ghar—house	چڑھ	chaṛh—climb
بھی	bhí—also, too	تھن	than—teat
دکھ	dukh—pain	رکھ	rakh—put, keep
کچھ	kuchh—some	پڑھ	paṛh—read
لکھ	likh—write	لوگ	log—people
تول	tol—weight	تھی	thí—was
تھے	the—were	کیل	kíl—nail
چیل	chíl—kite	نیک	nek—good
میز	mez—table	تیل	tel—oil

پیڑ per—tree	گرا girá—fell
ایک ek—one	تین tín—three
تیز tez—sharp	شیر sher—lion

[*Notes.*—(1) If there is a pesh over و and it gives long sound an ulṭá pesh is used for it as بو bú (smell). This و is called Ma'ruf. The و over which is a pesh and does not give long sound sídhá pesh is used for it as بو bo (sow). This و is called Majhúl.

(2) ي under which is zer and gives long sound mark of زیر is put under the dots as تیر tír (arrow) This ی is called Ma'rúf. The ی under which there is زیر and does not give long sound mark of زیر is understood as پیڑ per (tree). This is ی called Majhúl.]

LESSON 6.
Words of four combined letters.

دھوپ dhúp—sunlight	کتاب kitáb—book
ٹوپی ṭopí—cap, hat	دوات dawát—inkpot
میرا mera / میری merí / میرے mere —my, mine	چاقو cháqú—knife

دوڑنا	daurná—run	گلاب	guláb—rose
پھول	phúl—flower	پینا	píná—drink
پانی	pání—water	کھلا	khulá—open
تختی	taḳhtí—slate	برتن	bartan—pot, utensil
غلطی	ġalatí—mistake	صحیح	sahíh—right
گھوڑا	ghoṛá—horse	بھوک	bhúk—hunger
ریچھ	ríchh—bear	کھیت	khet—field
پیٹھ	piṭh—back	نفرت	nafrat—despise
گردن	gardan—neck	چہرہ	chihra—face
مغرب	maġrib—west	شمال	shimál—north
جنوب	junúb—south	لڑکا	laṛká—boy
خاص	ḳhás—principal, chief	صفت	sifat—quality
شخص	shaḳhs—person	جیسے	jaise—as
دوست	dost—friend	معنی	ma'ní—meaning

مِثَال misál—example | قَرِيب qaríb—near
بَعِيد ba'íd—far, distant | مَحَض mahaz—merely
ظَاهِر záhir—express | قَيدِى qaidí—prisoner
اِينٹ ínṭ—brick | اُونٹ úṇṭ—camel
هنسِي hansi—laughter | كوشِش koshish—effort
اُوپَر úpar—over, upon | نِيچے níche—down
نِهِين nahíṇ—na, not | سانپ sáṇp—snake
جُمله jumla—sentence | حَمله hamla—attack
مِحنَت mihnat—labour | مَسجِد masjid-mosque
فَارسِي Fársí—Persian | زَبَان zabán—language; tongue
نَظَر nazar—eye-sight | سَمجهه samajh—understanding

LESSON 7.

Alfáz ma'i Hamza, Tashdíd aur Nun gunna ke.

Words with Hamza, Tashdid and Nun gunna.

(ء) *Hamza*

لاؤ	láo—bring	کھائی	khái—ditch
آؤ	áo—come	جاؤ	jáo—go
گاؤ	gáo—cow	گانو	gán̲o—village
دکھاؤ	dikháo—show	کھلاؤ	khiláo—feed
ناؤ	náo—boat	گھٹاؤ	ghaṭáo—subtract
گائے	gáe—cow	آئے	áe—came
گئے	gae—went	بھائی	bhái—brother
روئی	ruí—cotton	نائی	nái—barber
گائیں	gáen̲—cows	آئیں	áin̲—came
ہوئیں	huín̲—became	دائی	dái—nurse
کوئی	koí—any, some	حلوائی	ha—halwai—confectioner
دوائی	dawái—medicine	صفائی	safái—cleanness
رہائی	rihái—deliverance	روشنائی	roshnái—ink

(ّ) *Tashdíd*

رسّی	rassí—rope	کچّا	kachchá—unripe, raw
سچّا	sachchá—truthful	بچّہ	bachcha—infant

گنّا ganná—sugarcane   چھرّا chharrá—small shots

اَچّھا achchhá—good   بِلّی billí—cat

پتّا pattá—leaf   بتّی battí—wick

شکّر shakkar—sugar   چکّی chakkí—mill

مٹّی maṭṭí—earth   حُقّہ huqqa—smoking-pipe

قِصّہ qissa—story   حِصّہ hissa—part

غُصّہ gussa—anger   کُتّا kuttá—dog

امّا ammá—mother   چمّچ chammach—spoon

کھٹّا khaṭṭá—sour   جُثّہ jussa—body

بُنّا bunná—weave   چچّا chachchá—uncle

چُنّا chunná—select   ٹٹّی ṭaṭṭí—fence, latrine

مکّھی makkhí—fly   سِلّی sillí—whet-stone

LESSON 8.

(ں) *Nùn̲ gunná*

[*Note.*—When the nasal sound of ں gunná in a word occurs between the other letters usual dot remains over its particle but nasal sound is understood.]

یہاں yahán̲—here	سینگ sín̲g—horn
ماں mán̲—mother	تمھیں tumhen̲—to you
ہیں hain̲—are	میں main̲—I
آنکھ án̲kh—eye	دانت dán̲t—tooth
سانڈ sán̲ḍ—bull	اُونٹ ún̲ṭ—camel
اُنھیں unhen̲—them	سانپ sán̲p—snake
بانس bán̲s—bamboo	کہیں kahín̲—somewhere
میں men̲—in	منہ mun̲h—mouth
سانس sán̲s—breath	اینٹ ín̲ṭ—brick
پانچ pán̲ch—five	کھانسی khán̲sí—cough
مانگ mán̲g—demand	ننگا nan̲gá—naked
پرند parin̲d—bird	باندی bán̲dí—slavegirl

کہاں جہاں kahán̲, jahán̲—where

Exercise.

Write Roman equivalents of :—

سَب پَر چُپ ہَم بُل

سے ہُو وُہ کُل لَو

کہ بو کر بس بط

کا دھوپ کھیت کتاب پھول

شخص بعید ظاہر نہیں نظر

تختی صحیح شمال جنوب مشرق

مغرب مسجد حملہ جملہ کھلا

شور صفت معنی مثال بھوک

طاق شام تین کچھ تھے

ہوش کھیل نمک گرا لاؤ

صفائی رہائی دائی جاؤ بھلائی

کھلاؤ کوئی کائے ہوئیں آئے

دکھاؤ روشنائی دوائی بچہ حقہ

شکر چکی متی غصہ اما

سلی مکھی بتی کتا گدا

اونٹ مُنھ بَانس مانگ تُمھیں

ہیں سہنگ یہاں نَنگا اینٹ

آنکھ مَیں کھانسی سانپ کہاں

باندی پرند مَیں مانگ سانگ

بانس دانت کھیں لڑکا

Write Urdu equivalents of :—

pás	log	the	tel	mez
tol	thí	girá	báp	nám
áyá	cháe	chaṛh	mor	chíl
dukh	hosh	náp	tez	sher
qism	jáu	mat	kam	tab
wuh	laṛ	sab	bú	ho
hár	kar	lo	mis	pul
jab	yih	tú	bad	ḳhat
dhúp	khet	laṛká	bartan	hansí
pání	gardan	mihnat	qaríb	cháqú
merá	dawát	kitáb	ṭopí	dauṛná
koshish	níche	samajh	Fársí	ríchh
píṭh	ḳhás	ba'íd	guláb	bhúk
bháí	gáe	dái	jáo	áo
huín	rihái	roshnái	náo	ruí
áín	huqqa	chammach	ṭaṭṭí	kachchá

pattá	rassí	chakkí	sillí	kuttá
ganná	shakkar	gussa	makkhí	billí
bachcha	main̲	khán̲sí	hain̲	mán̲
bán̲s	ún̲ṭ	dán̲t	sán̲s	sán̲ḍ
mun̲h	in̲ṭ	bán̲dí	án̲kh	nan̲gá

CHAPTER III.

Jumla or Fiqra or Kalám.

Sentence.

LESSON 1.

Two or more words so joined as to express thought form a Jumla (**sentence**).

A

SHORT SENTENCES.

tez chal—Walk fast.

qalam do—Give the pen.

مت ڈر mat ḍar—Do not fear.

دو دن رہ do din rah —Stay two days.

آج جا áj já—Go to-day.

یہہ پہل چکھہ yih phal chakh—Taste this fruit.

وہ خط پڑہ wuh ḳhat paṛh—Read that letter.

سچ بول sach bol—Speak the truth.

وہ آیا wuh áyá—He came.

گڑبڑ مت کر garbaṛ mat kar—Don't make confusion.

چپ رہ chup rah—Keep quiet.

تم ہو tum ho—You are.

میں ہوں maiṉ húṉ—I am.

یہہ ہل ہے yih hal hai—It is a plough.

لڑ مت laṛ mat—Don't fight.

پل پر جا pul par já—Go over the bridge.

اس کا باپ آیا uská báp áyá—His father came.

دھوپ تیز ہے dhúp tez hai—The sun is hot.

میرا چاقو تیز ہے merá cháqú tez hai—My knife is sharp.

ایک خط لکھو ek ḳhat likho—Write a letter.

اس کو ہوش نہیں ہے usko hosh nahín hai—He is not in sense.

میں نہیں چڑھ سکتا maiṉ nahíṉ chaṛh sakta—I cannot (can't) climb.

لوگ آتے اور جاتے ہیں log áte aur játe haiṉ—People come and go.

Exercise.

Read and write :—

تیز چل tez chal. قلم دو qalam do مت ڈر mat ḍar. آج جا áj já. دو دن رہ do din rah. وہ آیا wuh áyá. وہ خط پڑھ wuh khat paṛh. تم ہو tum ho. میں ہوں main húṉ لڑ مت laṛ mat. گڑبڑ مت کر gaṛbaṛ mat kar. پل پر جا pul par já. چپ رہ chup rah. دھوپ تیز ہے dhúp tez hai. یہہ پھل چکھہ yih phal chakh. یہہ ہل ہے yih hal hai. سچ بول sach bol. اسکا باپ آیا uská báp áyá. اسکو ہوش نہیں ہے usko hosh nahíṉ hai. میں نہیں چڑھ سکتا main nahíṉ chaṛh saktá.

Write Roman equivalents of :—

تیز چل - آج جا - وہ آیا - دو دن رہ - تم ہو -

یہہ ہل ہے - پل پر جا - چپ رہ - مت ڈر - گڑبڑ مت کر -

سچ بول - وہ خط پڑھ - اس کا باپ آیا - دھوپ تیز ہے -

یہہ پھل چکھہ - میں نہیں چڑھ سکتا - میرا چاقو تیز ہے -

لوگ آتے اور جاتے ہیں - ایک خط لکھو -

Write Urdu equivalents of :—

Mat ḍar, Wuh áyá. Tum ho. Qalam do Tez chal. Áj já. Chup rah. Maiṉ húṉ. Do din rah. Wuh ḳhat paṛh. Yih hal hai. Uská báp áyá. Dhúp tez hai. Sach bol. Pul par já. Log áte aur játe haiṉ. Merá cháqú tez hai. Ek ḳhat likho. Maiṉ nahíṉ chaṛh saktá. Usko hosh nahíṉ hai.

B.

SHORT LESSONS

For Reading and Writing.

LESSON 2.

[*Note.*—It is not necessary to mark the vowel points always. They are generally omitted after the Primary Lessons. Having been conversant with the language gradually you can read and utter the pronunciation of the words at first sight.]

پھُول باغ میں اُگتے ھیں Phúl bág meṉ ugte haiṉ —Flowers grow in the garden.

گائے ھمیں دن میں دو بار دودھ دیتی ھے Gáe hameṉ din meṉ do bár dúdh detí hai—The cow gives us milk twice a day.

ھندوستان گرم ملک ھے Hindustán garm mulk hai —India is a hot country.

تمہارے ھاتھہ میں کیا ھے ؟ Tumháre hath meṉ kyá hai ? —What is there in your hand ?

پھاٹک میں تالا لگادو Pháṭak men̲ tálá lagá do—Lock up the gate.

اُسکو دمہ کا عارضہ ھے Usko dama ká 'árza hai —He is suffering from Asthma.

یہہ کتاب رام پرشاد کی کتاب کے مانند ھے Yih kitáb Ram Parshad ki kitáb ke mánind hai—This book is like Ram Prasad's book.

دوست وہی ھے جو مصیبت کےوقت کام آوے Dost wuhí hai jo musíbat ke waqt kám áwe—A friend in need is friend indeed.

ھوا کے بغیر ھم زندہ نہیں رہ سکتے Hawá ke bagair ham zinda nahín̲ rah sakte–Without air we cannot live.

دروازہ پر کوئی کھڑا ھے Darwáze par koí khaṛá hai —Somebody is standing at the gate.

اُسکے ھاتھہ میں ایک لمبی چھڑی ھے Uske háth men̲ ek lambí chhaṛí hai—He has a long stick in his hand.

رات کو پرند اکثر درخت کی شاخ پر بیٹھتے ھیں Rát ko parind aksar darakht kí shákh par baiṭhte hain̲ —Birds often sit down, on a branch of tree at night.

LESSON 3.

میں اُسکی شادی کے وقت موجود تھا Main̲ uski shádí ke waqt maujúd thá—I was present at his marriage.

اُسکا انتقال بریلی میں ھوا Uská intiqál Bareilly men huá—He died at Bareilly.

سب لڑکیوں میں وہ حسین ھے Sab laṛkion men wuh hasín hai—She is the fairest of the girls.

میں کبھی اپنا وقت فضول ضایع نہیں کرتا Main kabhí apnà waqt fuzúl záya' nahín kartá—I never waste my time in vain.

تم مجھے ھمیشہ پڑھتے وقت دق کرتے ھو Tum mujhe hamesha parhte waqt diq karte ho—You always disturb me when I read.

احمق آدمی کی صحبت سے بچو Ahmaq ádmí kí suhbat se bacho —Avoid the company of fools.

جھوٹھے کا کوئی اعتبار نہیں کرتا Jhúṭhe ká koí e'tbár nahín kartá—None believes a liar.

یہہ شہنشاہ کي مہر ھے Yih Shahanshâh kí mohar hai—It is the seal of the King-Emperor.

تانبے کو سانچے میں ڈھالو Tànbe ko sánche men dhàlo—Cast the copper in the mould.

قیدی نے جرم کا اقرار کرلیا Qaidí ne jurm ká iqrár kar liyá—The prisoner confessed his crime.

وہ اُس وقت تك ميرا مطلب نہ سمجھا تھا Wuh us waqt tak merá matlab na samjhá thá—He had not understood my object up to that time.

LESSON 4.

ہم کانپور قبل آدھی رات کے پہونچینگے Ham Cawnpore qabl ádhí rát ke pahunchenge—We shall arrive at Cawnpore before midnight.

میں نے اپني بیٹي کو سونے کا ایك ھار دیا ھے Main ne apní beṭí ko sone ká ek hár diyá hai—I have given my daughter a gold necklace.

ھمارے جسم کا وہ حصہ جسمیں آنکھہ کان ناك اور منھہ ھے چہرہ کہلاتا ھے Hamáre jism ká wuh hissa jis men ánkh, kán, nák aur munh hai chehrá kahlátá hai—The part of our body with the eyes, the ears, the nose and the mouth is called the face.

گدّر امرود بہت ذائقہ دار ھوتے ھیں Gaddar amrúd bahut záiqadár hote hain—Half-ripe guavas are very tasteful.

پہاڑی لوگ چمڑے کی پوشاك پہنتے ھیں Pahárí log chamṛe kí poshák pahinte hain Mountaineers dress themselves with skin.

میرا وطن آگرہ ھے Merá watan Agra hai—My birthplace is Agra.

علم حاصل کرنے کی کوشش کرو 'Ilm hásil karne kí koshish karo—Try to acquire knowledge.

مجھے اُس سے کچھہ تعلق نہیں Mujhe us se kuchh ta'alluq nahín—I have no connection with him.

اُسکو اپنی دولت کا گھمنڈ ھے Usko apní daulat ká ghamand hai—He is proud of his wealth.

کیا تم تلوار چلانا جانتے ھو ؟ Kyá tum talwár chaláná jánte ho ?—Do you know how to use the sword ?

اُسنے میری بڑی خاطر تواضع کی Usne merí barí khátir tawazo' kí—He received me with great hospitality.

تجارت سب سے عمدہ پیشہ ھے Tijárat sab se 'umda pesha hai—Trade is the best occupation.

مالی ایک گلدستہ میرے لئے لایا ھے Málí ek guldasta mere liye láyá hai—The gardener has brought a bunch of flower for me.

کیا تم نے کبھی پریوں کا قصہ سنا ھے ؟ Kyá tum ne kabhí parion ká qissa suná hai ?—Have you ever heard a fairy tale ?

LESSON 5.

چند سال گذرے ایك میم غبارے میں اُڑي تھي Chand sál guzre ek mem gubbáṛe men̲ uṛí thí—Some years ago a lady had gone up in a balloon.

لچھمن نے گوپال کی جائداد پر قبضہ کرلیا Lachhman ne Gopál ki jáedád par qabza kar liyá—Lachhman took possession of Gopal's property.

میں تمکو اکثر سڑك پر گھومتے دیکھتا ھوں Main̲ tum ko aksar saṛak par ghúmte dekhtá hún̲—I often find you walking in the street.

میري گھڑی میں پانچ بجے ھیں Merí ghaṛí men̲ pán̲ch baje hain̲—It is five by my watch.

گذشتہ دوشنبہ سے بخار نہیں آتا Guzashta do-shamba se buk̲hár nahín̲ átá—There has been no fever since Monday last.

ھری موھن بابو مدعا علیہ کے وکیل تھے Harí Mohan Bábú mudd'a 'aleh ke vakíl the—Hari Mohan Babu was a pleader for the defendant.

میں تمکو اِس شرط پر معاف کرتا ھوں Main̲ tumko is shart par mu'áf kartá hún̲—I excuse you on this condition.

تبت ھند,ستان کے شمال میں ھے Tibbet Hindustán ke shimál meṉ hai—Tibet is to the north of India.

دروازہ پر کون دستک دیتا ھے Darwáze par kaun dastak detá hai—Who is knocking at the door?

میں مشکل سے چل سکتا ھوں Maiṉ mushkil se chal saktá húṉ—I can walk with difficulty.

تم کو بد دیانت نوکر کبھی نہ رکھنا چاھئے Tum ko bad diyánat naukar kabhí na rakhná cháhiye—You should never keep a dishonest servant.

اُسے اپنی پیر سالہ ماں کی خبر لینا چاھئے Use apni pírsála má kí ḳhabar lená cháhiye—He should take care of her aged mother.

میں خواہ مخواہ وھاں نہیں جا سکتا Maiṉ ḳhwáh maḳhwáh wahán̠ nahíṉ já saktá—I cannot go there without rhyme or reason.

میں تہہ دل سے آپکو پیار کرتا ھوں Maiṉ tah-i-dil se áp ko pyár kartá húṉ—I love you from the bottom of my heart.

وہ در حقیقت بہت نیک آدمی ھے Wuh dar ḥaqíqat bahut nek ádmí hai—He is really a very good man.

میں تمھارا معاملہ طے کرنے کے لئے حتی‌الامکان کوشش کرونگا Maiṉ tumhárá mu'ámila tai karne ke liye

hattul imkán koshish karúngá—I will try as far as possible to settle your case.

LESSON 6.

وہ تخمیناً دو سو روپیہ کا قرضدار ہے Wuh takhmínan do sau rupae ka qarzdár hai—He is in debt of approximately two hundred rupees.

ڈاکوؤں کا ایک گروہ یکایک گانوں میں نظر آیا

Ḍákuon ká ek guroh yakáyak gáon men nazar áyá—A band of robbers all of a sudden appeared in the village.

میرے رشتیدار بھی گانوں کو چھوڑ دینگے Mere rishtedár bhí gáno ko chhoṛ denge—My relatives will likewise leave the village.

تم نے یہہ جرم کیا لہذا تمکو اسکا نتیجہ اٹھانا ہوگا

Tum ne yih jurm kiyá lihází tumko uská natíja uṭháná hogá—You have committed this crime therefore you will have to suffer the consequences.

میرے دوست نے پیشتر یہہ رسالہ نہیں دیکھا تھا Mere dost ne peshtar yah risála nahín dekhá thá—My friend had not seen the pamphlet before.

لڑکوں کو اپنے والدین کا حکم ماننا چاہئے Laṛkon ko apne wálidain ka hukm mánná cháhiye—Children ought to obey their parents.

مشکل لفظوں کے معنے لغت میں دیکھو Mushkil lafzon ke ma'ne lugat men dekho—Find out the meanings of hard words in the Dictionary.

کمہار مٹي کے برتن بناتے هیں Kumhár miṭṭí ke bartan banáte hain—Potters make earthenware.

رات کو سوتے میں خواب دیکھنے کا کیا باعث هے Rát ko sote men ḳhwáb dekhne ká kyá bá'is hai—What is the cause of having dreams while sleeping in the night?

LESSON 7.

مُرغ ایک خوبصورت اور بہادُر پرَند هوتا هے - وہ کسي دوسرے پرند سے نہیں ڈرتا - بعض اوقات وہ دوسرے مرغوں سے لڑ جاتا هے - وہ گھڑي کا کام دیتا هے - همکو وقت بتلاتا هے - صبح جبکہ آفتاب طلوع هوتا هے وہ بانگ دیتا هے گویا همکو جتاتا هے کہ اب اُٹھنے کا وقت هے - مرغ خانگی پرند هے - مادہ کو مرغی کہتے هیں مرغي انڈے دیتی هے جنسے بچّے پیدا هوتے هیں وے چوزے کہلاتے هیں - انڈا اور چوزے کا شوربا مقوّي غذا هے - بہت لوگ مرغ مرغیاں پالتے هیں - جب مرغی کے انڈے کا وقت آتا هے تو وہ عموماً ایک انڈا هر روز دس یا پندرہ یا بیس دن تک دیتی هے -

Roman equivalent—

Murg ek khúbsùrat aur bahádur parind hotá hai. Wuh kisí dúsre parind se nahín dartá. Ba'z auqát wuh dúsre murgon se lar játá hai. Wuh gharí ká kám detá hai, hamko waqt batlátá hai. Subah jabki áftáb tulú' hotá hai, wuh báng detá hai goyá hamko jagátá hai ki ab uthne ká waqt hai. Murg khángí parind hai. Mádá ko murgí kahte hain. Murgí ande detí hai jinse bachche paidá hote hain, we chúze kahláte hain. Andá aur chúze ká shorbá muqawwì gizà hai. Bahut log murg aur murgì pàlte hain. Jab murgí ke andá dene ká waqt átá hai to wuh 'umùman ek andá har roz das yá pandrah, yá bìs dín tak detí hai.

English equivalent—

The cock is a fine and brave bird. He is not afraid of any other bird. Sometimes he fights with other cocks. He is as good as a clock. He tells us the time. The cock crows in the morning, when the sun rises, as if hê tells us it is time to get up. The cock is a domestic bird. The female is called hen (murgí). The hen lays eggs which produce little birdies. They are called chickens. The egg and the chicken broth are nourishing and invigorating food. Many people keep cocks and hens. When the time of laying eggs comes, she generally lays one egg daily for ten, fifteen or twenty days.

LESSON 8.

آفتاب هم کو روشني اور گرمي پهونچاتا هے جنکے بغیر هم زنده نهیں ره سکتے اور نه پودے بڑه سکتے هیں - پودے بغیر آفتاب کے سوکهه جاتے هیں - آفتاب هماری تندرستي کو قائم رکهتا هے - لوگ زرد پڑجاتے هیں اور مریض هوجاتے هیں اگر دهوپ اُنکے گهر میں نهیں آتی - ایك کهاوت هے " جهاں آفتاب کی روشني (دهوپ) کا دخل نهیں وهاں ڈاکٹر کا دخل ضرور هوتا هے - " آفتاب همکو مرضوں سے بچاتا هے کیونکه وه هوا کو اُن مادّوں سے جو هماري تندرستی پر اثر ڈالتے هیں اور مرض پیدا کردیتے هیں صاف رکهتا هے - اس لئے همکو اپنے مکانات اس طریقے سے بنانا چاهئے که انمیں تازی هوا اور آفتاب کي روشني (دهوپ) آتي رهے -

Roman equivalent—

Áftáb hamko roshní aur garmí pahunchátá hai jinke bagair ham zinda nahíṉ rah sakte aur na paude baṛh sakte haiṉ. Paude bagair áftáb ke súkh játe haiṉ. Áftáb hamári tandurustí ko qáim rakhtá hai. Log zard paṛ játe aur maríz ho játe haiṉ agar dhúp unke ghar meṉ nahíṉ átí. Ek kahâwat hai ki "Jaháṉ áftáb ki roshní (dhúp) ká daḵhl nahíṉ waháṉ Doctor ká daḵhl zarúr hotá hai." Áftáb hamko marzoṉ se bachátá hai kiyuṉki wuh hawá ko un máddoṉ se jo hamárí tandurustí par asar ḍálte haiṉ aur marz paidá kar dete haiṉ sáf rakhtá hai. Is liye hamko apne makánát is taríqe se banáná cháhiye ki un meṉ tází hawá aur áftáb kí roshní (dhúp) áti rahe.

English equivalent—

The sun gives us light and heat, without which we cannot live and plants cannot grow. Plants wither without the sun. The sun also keeps our health for people grow pale and sickly, if they do not allow the light of the sun to enter their houses. So we get the wise saying. "Where the sunlight cannot enter the Doctor must." It keeps us from disease because it makes the air free from those matters which tell heavily upon our health and thus bring about diseases. We must therefore build our houses in a way as to let in both fresh air and light of the sun.

LESSON 9.

بادشاہ شاندار عمارت میں رہتا ہے جسے محل کہتے ہیں - وہ بیش قیمت چیزیں پہنتا ہے اور لوگوں کی ایک بڑی تعداد پر حکومت کرتا ہے جو کہ رعایا کہلاتے ہیں-

فرماں رواٹی کے کام میں افسران جو کہ وزیر کہلاتے ہیں اسکی مدد کرتے اور صلاح دیتے ہیں - بادشاہ اپنے فرمانروا ملک کو دشمنوں سے محفوظ رکھنے کے لئے ایک طاقتور فوج رکھتا ہے - وہ ملک جسپر ایک بادشاہ حکومت کرتا ہے بادشاہت (سلطنت) کہلاتا ہے اور جن پر وہ حکومت کرتا ہے قوم کہلاتے ہیں - نیک بادشاہ کو رعایا پیار کرتی ہے - قوانین جو کہ بادشاہ جاری کرتا ہے عمل میں لائے جاتے ہیں کیونکہ لوگ ڈرتے ہیں کہ اگر تعمیل نہ کرینگے تو سزا دی جاویگی - بادشاہ کا فرض ہے کہ اپنی رعایا کی حفاظت کرے - بادشاہ رعایا پر محصول لگاتا ہے تاکہ انتظام حکومت کے ضروری اخراجات پورے کرسکے -

Roman equivalent—

Bádsháh shándár 'imárat men̲ rahtá hai jise Mahal kahte hain̲. Wuh beshqímat chízen̲ pahintá hai aur logon̲ kí baṛí ta'dád par hukúmat kartá hai jo ki ri'áyá kahláte hain̲. Farmán̲rawáí ke kám men̲ afsarán jo ki Wazír kahláte hain̲ uskí madad karte aur saláh dete hain̲. Bádsháh apne farmán̲rawá mulk ko dushmanon̲ se mahfúz rakhne ke liye ek táqatwar fauj rakhtá hai. Wuh mulk jis par ek bádsháh hukúmat kartá hai bádsháhat (saltanat) kahlátá hai aur log jin par wuh hukúmat kartá hai Qaum kahláte hain̲. Nek bádsháh ko ri'áyá pyár kartí hai. Qawánín jo ki Bádsháh járí kartá hai 'ámal meṉ láe játe haiṉ kiyuṉki log ḍarte haiṉ ki agar ta'mil na kareṉge to sazá dí jáwegí. Bádsháh ká farz hai ki apní ri'áyá kí hifázat kare. Bádsháh ri'áya par mahsúl lagátá hai táki intizám-i-hukúmat ke zarùrí iḵhráját púre kar sake.

English equivalent—

A King lives in a magnificent building called a *palace.* He wears jewels and rules over a large number of people called his subjects. In the task of government he is assisted by officers called ministers who give him their advice. A king has a strong army to defend the country over which he reigns against enemies. The country over which a king rules is called kingdom and the people whom he rules called a nation. A good king is loved by his subjects. The laws which a king makes are obeyed because people fear the punishment which will be inflicted on them if they do not obey them. It is the duty of a king to see that his subjects are safe. A king makes his subjects pay taxes to provide him with the money necessary to carry on the work of Government.

LESSON 10.

ھندوستان کے عجائبات میں برگد کا درخت کچھ
کم عجوبہ چیز نہیں ہے اسکو دیکھتے ھی یہ درخت

نخلستان یا درختوں کا کنج سا نظر آتا ہے - ایسا ایک بڑا بھاری درخت لنکا میں ہے جسکے سایہ تلے سؤ جھونپڑیوں کا ایک گانو بسا ہے - ایک درخت میں ۳۵۰ بڑے اور تین ہزار چھوٹے تنے گنے گئے ہیں - کہتے ہیں کہ ایک برگد کے درخت کے نیچے پانچ ہزار آدمیوں کی فوج نے پڑاؤ ڈالا تھا - یہہ تعجب ہے کہ ایک اکیلا تنا جو کہ پہلے بیج سے نکلا ایک نخلستان ہو جاوے - اسکی ایسی لمبی اور بھاری شاخیں ہوتی ہیں کہ انکا پھیلا رہنا بغیر کسي تھونی یا سہارے کے غیر ممکن معلوم ہوتا ہے - قدرت اسکو تھونیاں مہیا کرتی ہے - جیوں جیوں شاخیں لمبائی اور وزن میں بڑھتی جھوتے کلّے انمیں سے پھوٹ نکلتے ہیں - نیچے کی طرف بڑھتے ہیں اور آخر کار زمین تک پہونچ جاتے ہیں - وے مٹی میں بیٹھہ جاتے ہیں اور چاروں طرف جڑیں پھینک دیتے ہیں اس طرح مضبوطی سے جڑ پکڑ لیتے ہیں - تب وے موٹے ہوجاتے ہیں اور مضبوط تنے بن جاتے ہیں - یہہ تنے ان شاخوں کو جن سے وے اصل میں نکلے ہیں تھامے رہتے ہیں - پتیاں ایسي گھنی ہوتی ہیں کہ مشکل سے بارش کا پانی اسمیں سے گرتا ہے - آفتاب کی روشنی اسمیں نہیں گھس سکتي - دن کے وقت بھی گودھولی سي رہتی ہے -

Roman equivalent—

Hindustán ke 'ajáibát men̲ bargad ká daraḵht kuchh kam 'ajúba chíz nahín̲ hai. Usko dekhte hì yih daraḵht naḵhlistán yá daraḵhton̲ ká kuñj sá nazar átá hai. Aisá ek baṛá bhárí daraḵht Lanká men̲ hai jiske sáya tale sau jhopṛíon̲ ká ek gáon̲ basá hai. Ek daraḵht men̲ 350 baṛe aur tín hazár chhoṭe tane gine gae hain̲. Kahte hain̲ ki ek bargad ke daraḵht ke níche 5 hazár ádmion̲ ki fauj ne paṛáo dálá thá. Yih ta'jjub hai ki ek akelá taná jo ki pahle bíj se niklá thá ek naḵhlistán hojáwe. Us kí aisí lambí aur bhári sháḵhen̲ hotí hain̲ ki unká phailá rahna bagair kisí sahàre yá thùnì ke gair mumkin m'lùm hotá hai. Qudrat usko thúnián̲ muhaiyá kartí hai. Jyon̲ jyun̲ sháḵhen̲ lambáí aur wazn men̲ baṛhtí játí hain̲ chhoṭe kille unmen̲ se phùṭ nikalte hain̲. We níche kí taraf baṛhte hain̲ aur áḵhir kár zamín tak pahun̲ch játe hain̲ We miṭṭí men̲ baiṭh játe hain̲ aur chárón̲ taraf jaṛen̲ phenk dete hain̲ is tarah mazbùtí se jaṛ pakaṛ lete hain̲. Tab we moṭe ho játe hain̲ aur mazbút tane ban játe hain̲. Yih tane un sháḵhon̲ ko jin se we asl men̲ nikle hain̲ tháme rahte hain̲. Pattián̲ aisí ghani hotí hain̲ ki mushkil se bárish ká pání usmen̲ se girtá hai. Aftáb kí roshni usmen̲ nahín̲ ghus saktí. Din ke waqt bhí godhúlì sí rahtí hai.

English equivalent :—

Of the many wonders to be found in India not the least wonderful is the banyan tree. At first sight the tree looks like a large grove. Such a gigantic tree is in Ceylon under whose shade stands a village of hundred huts. As many as three hundred and fifty large stems and three thousand smaller ones have been counted in one tree. It is said that an army of five thousand men once encamped under the shade of a single banyan. It is wonderful that the first single stem that springs from the seed becomes a grove. Its branches springing from the main trunk are so very long and heavy that it is impossible for them to remain stretched out, without some sort of prop or support. Props are provided by nature. As the branches increase in length and weight, little shoots spring from them, grow downwards and at last reach the ground. They find their way into the soil, send out rootlets on all sides, and thus take firm hold. Then they begin to grow thicker and stronger until they form strong stems. These stems hold up the branches from which they originally spring. The leaves grow so thick that rain hardly comes through. The sun's light cannot penetrate them. Even during the day-time we are in dim twilight.

LESSON II.

[*Read without the help of Roman*]

کفایت شعاری—*Kifáyat-sha'árí*

Frugality.

بعض آدمیوں کو اپنے بزرگوں (Ancestors—buzurgon) کی میراث (heritage—mírás) اِس قدر مل جاتی ھے - کہ وہ اُسکی آمدنی سے بغیر محنت کے اپنا گذارہ بخوبی کرسکتے ھیں - لیکن دنیا میں زیادہ تر ایسے آدمي ھیں جو اپنی ذاتی (Personal—zátí) محنت کی اُجرت (Wages—ujrat) سے اوقات بسر کرتے ھیں (Subsist—Auqát basar karte hain).

میراث کی آمدني یا اپني اُجرت کی محنت سے وھی لوگ فائدہ اٹھاتے ھیں جو نیك چلن اور دور اندیش (Farseeing—dúr andesh) ھوتے ھیں - کیونکہ نیك چلني انسان کو معاش (Livelihood, Bread—ma'ásh) پر آمادہ اور دوراندیشي خرچ کرنے کا طریقہ سکھاتی ھے -

دوراندیش آدمی آمد وخرچ کو اپني نظر میں رکھتا ھے - وہ آگے اور پیچھے دونوں طرف دیکھتا رھتا ھے - وہ بے ضرورت خرچ کرنے کو سخت گناہ جانتا ھے اگر آمدنی کم ھوتی ھے تو اپني ضرورتوں کو مختصر (Curtail—mukhtasar) کردیتا ھے حتی الامکان (As far—hattul-imkán as possible) کچھ نہ کچھ بچاتا ھے تاکہ بیکاری

(Illness—bímárí) بیماري — (Unemployment—bekárí) (Accidental—ittifáqí) اور اتفاقی (Famine—qahat) قحط ضرورتوں کے وقت کام آئے - وہ موقع پر دوسروں کی دستگیری کرتا ھے - ایسا آدمي کفایت شعار (Aid—dastgírí) کہلاتا ھے - (Frugal—Kifáyat-sha'ár)

LESSON 12.

صبر *Sabr*—Patience.

ایک سوداگر بازار سے سوار ھوا گھر واپس جا رھا تھا اپنے پیچھے ایک تھیلا لادے ھوئے جسمیں بہت روپیہ تھا- مینھہ (Rain—meṉh) کثرت سے برسا اور وہ آدمی بالکل تر ھوگیا - اس سے اُسکو بہت تکلیف ھوئی اور اُسنے موسم —shikáyat kí) کی شکایت کی (Weather—mausim) جو ایسے وقت میں خراب ھوا جبکہ اُسکا (Complained سفر کرنا لازمی تھا (Was obliged—lázmí thá)

اُسکا گذر ایک گنجان جنگل (gunján jaṉgal—) میں ھوا - خوف کی بات ھے کہ جیسے ھی (Thick forest وہ اسمیں داخل ھوا اُسنے ایک ڈاکو کو دیکھا جسنے اسکي طرف بندوق سے نشانہ لگایا - اسکا اسي جگھہ خاتمہ ھوگیا ھوتا لیکن مینھہ نے بارود (bárúd— کو ایسا نم کردیا تھا کہ بندوق نہ چلی (Gunpowder

مسافر نے گھوڑے کے ایڑ ماري (Put spurs—eṛ márí) اور
Escaped the—k̲hatre se pár ho gayá) خطرہ سے پار ھو گیا ۔
(danger - جبکہ وہ محفوظ جگھہ میں تھا اُسنے خیال کیا
کہ میں کیسا بے وقوف (Foolish—bewaqúf) تھا کہ
میں نے خراب موسم کی شکایت کي بجاے صبر کے ساتھہ
(Bearing—bardásht) برداشت (Patiently—sabr ke sáth)
کرنے کے گویا خدا کي طرف سے ھے - اگر آسمان صاف ھوتا
اور ھوا خشک تو میں اس وقت مردہ پڑا ھوتا اور میري بي بي
اور بچے میری آمد کا بے فائدہ انتظار کرتے ھوتے -
مینھہ نے جسکی کہ میں نے شکایت کي تھی میری جان اور
مال دونوں کی حفاظت کی آیندہ کو میں اس مقولہ
Forget—farámosh) کو ھرگز فراموش (Proverb—maqúla)
نکرونگا -

مقولہ — قبول کر خوشی سے جو اللہ تجھکو دیوے
بھتر ھے واسطے تیرے گو ظاھر ایسا نہ ھووے

LESSON 13.
نظم—*Nazm.*
Poem.

کسي بیکس کو اے بیداد گر مارا تو کیا مارا
جو آپ ھي مر رھا ھو اُس کو گر مارا تو کیا مارا
نہ مارا آپکو جو خاک ھو اکسیر ھو جاتا
اگر پارے کو اے اکسیر گر مارا تو کیا مارا

بڑے موزی کو مارا نفس امارہ کو گر مارا
نہنگ و اژدھا و شیر نر مارا تو کیا مارا
ھنسی کے ساتھہ یاں روتا ھے مثل قلقل مینا
کسي نے قہقہہ اے بے خبر مارا تو کیا مارا
گیا شیطان مارا ایک سجدہ کے نہ کرنے میں
اگر لاکھوں برس سجدہ میں سرمارا تو کیا مارا
دل بدخواہ میں تھا مارنا یا چشم بدبیں میں
فلک پر 'ذوق' تیر آہ گر مارا تو کیا مارا

سیر کر دنیا کی غافل زندگانی پھر کہاں
زندگي گر کچھہ رھي تو نوجوانی پھر کہاں

گلستان جہاں میں پھول بھی ھیں اور کانٹے بھی
مگر جو گل کے جویا ھیں انھیں کھا خار کا کھٹکا

جبکہ دو موذیوں میں ھو کھٹ پٹ
اپنے بچنے کي فکر کر جھٹ پٹ

PART II.

CHAPTER IV

لفظوں كي قسميں يا کلموں کی تقسیم

Classification of Words or Parts of Speech.

By careful study and exercise of the lessons given in Part I, one can be able to read, write and understand the language, but not fully, without the Grammar. In this Part II principles and rules of Grammar are treated for the right use of the Urdu language.

It is essential to know well the kinds or classes of words and the way of the formation of a word form another.

1. There are two ways of forming a word from another. One is called إشتقاق **Derivation** and the other گردان **Inflection**.

(1) اشتقاق **Derivation** changes the kind of

words, as گھر house (name of a place); گھریلو—household, domestic (the quality of the thing which lives in the house); شہر shahar (name of a place); شہري shahrí (the quality of the one who lives in the city, etc.)

(2) گردان—**Inflection** changes the تعداد Number of a word, as کتاب book is the name of one thing; کتابیں books is the name of more than one thing; لڑکی girl, لڑکیاں girls.

2. Some words such as هم we, دس ten, کلکته Calcutta, گاڑي carriage, گوپال Gopal, رونا weeping etc., etc. give their meanings without the help of another word. They are called اسم مطلق **Names in general**. But some words do not give meanings without the help of another word such as پس so, لیکن but, پر on, هیں are, سے from, etc. They are called حرف ربط **Connecting particles**.

(1) Some اسم مطلق **Names in general** are the names of persons, places, things and actions. They are called اسم **Nouns**.

(2) Some words, as دس ten, اچھا good, کالا black,

etc. describe the nature and quality of a Noun and they are called صفت **Adjectives.**

(3) Some words, as هم we, تم you, وہ he, میں I, اُسکا his, etc. are used in place of a Noun. They are called ضمیر **Pronouns.**

(4) Some words, such as گیا went, آتا ہے comes, گرا fell, show 'being and doing' of an action at some time. They are called فعل **Verbs.**

(5) Some words, such as تک till, کو to, پر on, کا of, ساتھہ with etc. are used to show relation of one thing with the other. They are called حرف ربط **Prepositions.**

(6) Some words, as اب now, تب then, وہاں, there, یہاں here etc. show time, place and (تاکید) emphasis about some work. They are called صلہ فعل **Adverbs.**

(7) Some words, as پس so, مگر but, اگر if, پھر again, join two words or sentences. They are called حرف عطف **Conjunctions.**

(8) Some words, such as ارے O, آؤ come, ہاے Oh etc., are used in calling to somebody and also in expressing sudden feelings and emotions of a person. They are called حرف صدا **Interjections.**

Thus there are eight kinds of words in the Urdu language. They are :—

اسم—**Noun.**	صلہ فعل—**Adverb.**
صفت—**Adjective.**	حرف ربط—**Preposition.**
ضمیر—**Pronoun.**	حرف عطف—**Conjunction.**
فعل—**Verb.**	حرف صدا—**Interjection.**

I.—اسم The NOUN.

تعریف اور قسمیں Definition and Kinds.

A Noun is the name of a person, place, thing or action, as جواهر لال Jawahir Lal, قلم pen, چاقو knife, سجاوت decoration, مدرسه school, الهآباد Allahabad, سلیٹ slate, کچهری court, کهیلنا play, دوڑنا run.

Main kinds of Nouns are three, namely :—

(1) جامد—**Simple Noun.**

(2) مصدر—**Primitive Noun.**

(3) مشتق—**Derivative Noun.**

(1) جامد **Simple Nouns** are those which neither themselves are formed from other words nor other words can be derived from them, as لڑکا boy موهن Mohan, لڑکی girl, آگره Agra, دهلی Delhi, etc.

(2) مصدر **Primitive Nouns** are those which

are not derived from some other words but other Nouns are derived from them, as سونا to sleep, گانا to sing, جانا to go, کرنا to do, etc. Sign of مصدر is the word نا (ná) at the end of the word.

(3) مشتق **Derivatives** are those which are derived from مصدر (Primitive Nouns) as from لکھنا to write, لکھنے والا writer, from جانا to go, جانے والا goer, from سجانا to decorate, سجاوٹ decoration.

(1)—جامد **Simple Nouns** are of two kinds :—

(*a*) اسم معرفہ یا خاص Proper Noun.

(*b*) اسم نکرہ یا عام Common Noun.

A.—معرفہ یا اسم خاص Proper Noun.

A معرفہ یا اسم خاص **Proper Noun** denotes only one person, place or thing, which distinguishes from all others, as موتی چند Moti Chand, مدراس Madras, ایفریقہ Africa, کوہ نور Koh-i-Noor, etc.

Besides the real names there are some other names which are taken as اسم خاص (**Proper Noun**).

(*a*) تخلص **Poetical name** – a short name used by Poets in their poems instead of their full names, as غالب Ghalib, سودا Sauda, حالی Hali, etc.

(*b*) خطاب Title—a name of honour offered by

Kings, as راے بہادر Rae Bahadur, خان بہادر Khan Bahadur, ایم - اے M. A. etc.

(c) لقب **Appellation**—a name famous on account of some special qualification, as اسفندیار پہلوان Isfandyár Pahlawán is called "روئیں تن Roeʼntan" etc.

(d) عُرف *alias*—**Famous name**—the other or the half name of a person which becomes famous for no reasons, as بیہریا Behariya from Behari Lal, رتنا Ratna from Ratan Chand, etc.

(e) کُنیّت **Connected name**—a name which is used in connection of the parents and children, as ابن مریم Ibn-i-Mariam ; ابن آدم Ibn-i-Adam etc. Females also call their husbands referring their children, they do not utter forth their names, as لچھمن کے بابو Lachhman ke Bábú, موہن کے لالہ Mohan ke Lala, etc

B.—نکرہ یا اسم عام Common Noun

اسم عام **Common Noun** is one that denotes any individual of a particular class or kind, as گھوڑا horse, کتا dog, انسان man etc. Common Nouns are مصدر Primitives as well as مشتق Derivatives.

اسم عام Common Nouns are of two kinds :—

(1) اسم ذات Concrete Noun.

(2) اسم صفات Abstract Noun.

1.—اسم ذات Concrete Noun.

اسم ذات **Concrete Noun** denotes something that has an actual and separate existence, as جان John گھرو house, گھوڑا horse, میز table, فوج army, قینچی scissors, etc.

اسم ذات—Concrete Nouns are divided into four classes :—

(1) اسم ذات مطلق—Simple Concrete Noun.

2) اسم آلہ Instrumental Noun.

(3) اسم ظرف Nouns of Time and Place.

(4) اسم جمع Collective Noun.

(1) اسم ذات مطلق **Simple Concrete Nouns** are the names of all the living and lifeless things.

(2) اسم آلہ **Instrumental Nouns** are the names of instruments, as چاقو knife, قینچی scissors, بسولہ adge, هل plough.

Some اسم آلہ Instrumental Nouns are made of Hindi, Persian or Arabic Verbs, as بیلن belan from the Hindi word بیلنا belná ; لٹکن laṭkan from لٹکنا laṭakná ; اُسترا usturá from the Persian Verb اُستردن ustardan (مونڈنا) ; پیمانہ from پیمودن paimúdan (ناپنا) ; مقراض miqráz (قینچی) from قرض qarz (کترنا); میزان mízán from وزن wazn (تول)

Some اسم آلہ Instrumental Nouns are formed by adding the Persian فعل Verb to some other noun, as رومال rúmál (handkerchief) = رو rú means منھ muṉh (face) and مال mál from مصدر Primitive noun, مالیدن málídan (ملنا malná—rub), the whole means "منھ پونچھنے کی چیز muṉh poṉchhne kí chíz"—the thing for wiping face. Similarly دوربین telescope, قلم تراش penknife, etc.

Some اسم آلہ Instrumental Nouns are formed of اسم ذات مطلق Simple Concrete Nouns, as ھتھوڑا from ھاتھ hand ; نکیل nakel from ناک nose ; داتون dáṉtaun from دانت tooth.

(3) اسم ظرف **Nouns of Time and Place** are the names of place or time, as آج to-day مدرسہ school, etc. [Names of places are called ظرف مکان and those of time ظرف زمان - ظرف مکان Nouns of Place are—بازار market ; دوکان shop ; شہر city ; گاؤں

village ; میدان plain etc. ظرف زمان Nouns of Time are—منهہ mouth ; رات night ; کل tomorrow ; دن day].

(i) Some ظرف مکان **Nouns of Place** are formed by adding آل ál, شالہ shála, واڑی wáṛí etc. to the Hindi words, as سسرال husband's house ; پاتھہشالہ school, پھلواڑی flower-garden etc.

(ii) Some are formed by adding ستان stán, گاہ gáh, شن shan, خانہ khána to the Persian Nouns, as گلستان flower-garden, خوابگاہ sleeping-room, گلشن orchard, کُتب خانہ library.

(iii) Some Arabic اسم ظرف are also used in Urdu, as مدرسہ school, مجلس meeting, مکتب academy.

(4) اسم جمع **Collective Noun** denotes a number of persons or things taken as one, as فوج army ; جھنڈ flock ; بھیڑ crowd, etc.

2.—اسم صفات Abstract Noun.

All the مشتق Derivatives are اسم صفات Abstract Nouns. They are of two kinds, (*a*) حاصل مصدر **Verbal Noun,** (*b*) حاصل صفت **Abstract Noun.**

(a) حاصل مصدر Verbal Noun.

حاصل مصدر Verbal Noun is the name of the effect or state of a فعل Verb, as دوڑ race is the effect of the Verb دوڑنا run ; سجاوٹ decoration is the state of the Verb سجانا decorate.

Some Rules for formation of. Verbal Nouns:

There is no particular rule in Urdu for making Verbal Nouns. Following are some easy rules :—

(i) Omit the particle نا ná the sign of مصدر Primitive Noun and the remaining portion is حاصل مصدر Verbal Noun, as from مارنا to strike, مار stroke ; from دوڑنا to run, دوڑ race etc.

(ii) Sometimes after removing the sign of مصدر Primitive, الف alif is added, as from رگڑنا ragaṛná رگڑا ragṛá ; from جھگڑنا jhagaṛná جھگڑا jhagṛá.

(iii) Sometimes deleting the sign of مصدر Primitive ن nún is added, as جلن jalan (burning) from جلنا to burn ; سوجن (swelling) from سوجنا to swell etc.

(*iv*) Sometimes omitting the sign of مصدر ،'و' vao is used, as لگاؤ lagáo from لگانا lagáná ; دباؤ pressure from دبانا to press.

(*v*) Sometimes آئی ái is added after removing the sign of مصدر, as سلائی sewing from سلانا to sew ; لڑائی fighting from لڑنا to fight.

(*vi*) Sometimes dropping the sign of مصدر وت vaṭ is added, as بناوت construction from بنانا to construct ; لکھاوت writing from لکھنا to write.

The Persian حاصل مصدر Verbal Nouns, such as اندیشہ fear ; کوشش effort ; شمار number, بخشش gift, etc. are also used without any change in their original forms.

(*b*) حاصل صفت Abstract Noun.

حاصل صفت Abstract Noun is the name of the effect and state of a Common Noun, as سچ truth is the effect of being true ; سیدھاپن gentleness is the state of being سیدھا gentle.

Rules for the formation of Abstract Noun.

(1) Drop ا alif at the end of an Adjective and the remainder shall be حاصل صفت Abstract Noun, as کھوت defect from کھوتا defective ; متاپا fatness from موتا fat etc.

(2) Sometimes اسم صفت is made by adding some letters instead of dropping of ا alif, as چھوتائي smallness from چھوتا small ; سڑاهت rottenness from سڑا rot etc.

(3) Sometimes by adding یاے معروف long ي ye to the adjective, as کنجوسي miserliness, misery from کنجوس miser ; مئےنوشی drinking from مئےنوش drunk or drunkard etc.

(4) Some are formed by adding پن pan at the end of an Adjective as بیواپن widowhood from بیوه widow, کنوارپن virginhood or virginity from کنواري virgin, etc.

(5) حاصل صفت Abstract Noun from Persian and Arabic صفت Adjective is formed by adding یاے معروف long ي after it, as نیکي goodness from نیک good, بهتري betterment from بهتر better ; امیری richness from امیر rich etc.

(2)—مصدر Primitive Noun or Root.

مصدر Primitive Noun or Root is that which denotes being, doing or enduring without any tense or time, as بنانا to make ; خریدنا to buy ; کھانا to eat ; غصہ ہونا to be angry ; شور کرنا to make noise etc.

The sign of مصدر Root in Urdu is نا ná but some words ending in نا ná are not مصدر Roots, as نانا grandfather, کانا one-eyed, چونا lime, گنا ganná etc.

Some مصدر Roots are formed from Hindi words, as دوڑنا to run ; بنانا to make ; کھانا to eat. These are called مصدر اصلی یا وضعی Real Roots.

Some are made by adding Hindi مصدر Root or its sign to the Persian and Arabic words, as شور کرنا to make noise ; غصہ ہونا to be angry ; خریدنا to buy etc. These are called مصدر بناوٹی یا غیروضعی Fictitious Roots.

Thus by the formation point of view مصدر Roots are of two kinds اصلی Real and بناوٹي Fictitious

By the meaning point of view there are two kinds of مصدر Roots:—

1. مصدر لازم **Intransitive.**

2. مصدر متعدی **Transitive.**

1. مصدر لازم **Intransitive** is that Root from which whatever فعل Verbs are formed they want only a فاعل (doer) Nominative, as سوھن آیا ھے Sohan has come. Here سوہن Sohan is فاعل Nominative and آیا ھے (has come) is Verb.

2. مصدر متعدي **Transitive** is that Root from which whatever Verbs are formed they want فاعل Nominative and مفعول Objective both, as ھیرا نے لچھمن کو مارا Hira struck Lachhman. Here ھیرا is فاعل Nominative, مارا is فعل Verb and لچھمن is Objective.

By the objective point of view there are three sorts of مصدر متعدي Transitive Roots :—

(1) Having one مفعول Objective, as کھانا eat ; پینا drink ; مارنا strike etc.

(2) Having two مفعول Objectives, as کھلانا feed; دینا give etc.

(3) Having three مفعول Objectives, as دلوانا dilwáná ; کھلوانا khilwáná ; پڑھوانا paṛhwáná etc.

By the formation point of view مصدر متعدي Transitive Roots are of two kinds :—

(1) متعدی بنفسہ اصلی Real Transitive, as کھانا eat ; لکھنا write ; پڑھنا read which are original.

(2) متعدی بالواسطہ Causative, as کھلونا cause to eat, بلوانا bulwáná etc. which are formed from مصدر Roots.

II. اسم کی گردان Inflection of Nouns.

To show the جنس Gender, تعداد Number and حالت Case of Nouns some changes occur and these changes are called گردان Inflection.

A.—(تذکیر , تانیث) جنس Gender.

Gender is that form of the Noun which shows whether what is spoken of is *male*, *female* or *neither.*

There are two Sexes—the نر *male* sex and the مادہ *female* sex.

(1) The names of males are of the مذکر Masculine Gender.

(2) The names of females are the مونث **Feminine Gender.**

(3) The names of things without life are of بےجان یا جنس غیر حقیقی **Neuter Gender,** *i. e.* neither masculine nor feminine.

(4) Words applied to both sexes are said to be of the جنس مشترک **Common Gender.**

Rules to find out جنس Genders.

1. **Masculine.—**

(1) Nouns ending in ' ا ' alif are often Masculine, as گھوڑا horse, بیٹا son, لڑکا boy, تماشا fun etc., but مالا wreath, چھالیا betel-nut, قبا dress, گھٹا clouds are Feminine.

(2) Nouns ending in ' ہ ' he are masculine if they are Neuter, as پردہ curtain, محکمہ department, صدمہ shock, مباحثہ discussion etc.

(3) All the Urdu Primitive Nouns or Roots are masculine.

(4) Hindi Verbal Nouns ending in ' ا ' alif or ' و ' vao are masculine, as جھگڑا quarrel, بہاؤ flow etc.

(5) Names of months and days and the word جاڑا járá (winter, cold) are masculine.

(6) Names of Natural objects such as سورج sun, چاند moon, ستارے stars, سیارے planets are masculine, as سورج نکلا The sun rose, چاند ڈوب گیا The moon set, etc.

2. Feminine.—

(1) Nouns ending in یاے معروف long ی ye are Feminine, as مرغی hen, بکری she-goat, گھوڑي mare, موری drain, کرسی chair etc. but گھی ghee, دھي curd, موتي pearl, پاني water etc. are masculine.

(2) Arabic Nouns ending in 'ہ' he are Feminine, as ملکہ queen, معلمہ tutoress, زوجہ wife etc.

(3) Arabic words such as تحریر writing, تعریف praise, تدبیر plan, contrivance تقصیر fault تعمیل execution, تقدیر destiny are Feminine but تعویز amulet, charm, is Masculine.

(4) Arabic Primitive Nouns or Roots ending in 'ا' alif or 'ت' te are Feminine, as قضا fate, جفا oppression, دغا fraud, غفلت

negligence, شدت intensity, عزت honour etc.

(5) Hindi Verbal Nouns not ending in 'ا' or 'و' váo and often the Persian Verbal Nouns are Feminine, as کوشش effort, بخشش gift, سفارش recommendation, رفتار speed, گفتگو conversation, سوجن swelling, هنسي laughter etc.

(6) The letters ب پ ت ٹ ث ج چ ح خ د ڈ ذ ر ز ژ ط ظ ف و ہ ي are Feminine, the rest are Masculine.

(7) The words تاریخ date, گرمی heat, برسات rains, هوا air are Feminine.

Rules for the Genders of some English Words used daily in Urdu conversation.

There is no mention of sex in the Neuter Nouns in English, but in Urdu there are rules for the sex of the neuter Nouns :—

(1, In English اسم جمع Collective Nouns are Neuter but if they are used in Urdu they are Feminine, as

کمیٹی Committee, کمپنی Company, پارلیمنٹ Parliament, کونسل Council.

(2) If there is a word in Urdu for the English Neuter Nouns and both are in use the Gender of the English word shall be the same as of Urdu, as آفس Office, پریس Press, باکس Box, پوسٹ آفس Post Office, etc. are spoken of as masculine because the Urdu words for them are masculine but واسکٹ, Waistcoat, گورنمنٹ Government, etc. are spoken of as Feminine.

(3) The Gender of the English words for which there is no Urdu word shall be somewhat the same as of names of similar things, as تکمہ Button, انگرکھا Coat, خزنہ Case, دیئا Lamp etc. But بوتل Bottle, مانسون Monsoon کمشن Commission, مشین Machine, چمنی Chimney لالٹین Lantern are Feminine because in Urdu نلي - کل - دستوري - هوا - شيشی شمع are Feminine.

Rules to form Feminine from Masculine.

Feminines can be formed from Masculines of living beings only.

(1) Masculines ending in 'ا' alif, 'ا' alif is changed into یاے معروف long ye, as:

كنوارا bachelor	كنواري maid, spinster
بچهيرا colt	بچهيري filly
مرغا cock	مرغي hen
بكرا he-goat	بكرى she-goat
گدها he ass	گدهي she-ass
گهوڙا horse	گهوڙى mare
لڑكا boy	لڑكي girl
بيٹا son	بيٹي daughter.

etc., etc.

(2) Some Masculines ending in 'ا' alif, 'ا' alif is changed into يا yá, as:

كتا dog	كتيا bitch
چڑا cock-sparrow	چڑيا hen-sparrow
چوها mouse	چوهيا she-mouse
بچهوا he-calf	بچهيا she-calf
بڑها old man	بڑهيا old woman

(3) Masculines not ending in 'ا' alif یاے معروف 'ی' ye or نی ní or آنی ání is added, as:

ڈوم a man of Hindu low caste	ڈومنی a woman of Hindu low caste

شیر lion	شیرنی lioness
سور boar	سورنی sow
هرن buck	هرنی doe
کبوتر male-pigeon	کبوتری female-pigeon
مهتر sweeper	مهترانی sweepress
نوکر man-servant	نوکرانی maid-servant

(4) Masculines ending in ی ' یاے معروف ' ye, ی is changed into ن as :

دھوبی washer-man	دھوبن washer-woman
درزی seamster	درزن seamstress
نائی man-barber	نائن female-barber
موچی male-shoe-maker	موچن female-shoe-maker

(5) Some Masculines are formed by adding ن nún as :

بلوچی male inhabitant of Baluchistan	بلوچن female inhabitant of Baluchistan
ناگ male serpent	ناگن female serpent

(6) Some Birds without any alteration are called Masculine or Feminine, as :

گد—vulture, آلو—owl are called Masculine.

چیل—kite, مینا—maina are called Feminine.

B.—(وحدت , جمعیت) تعداد Number.

There are only two Numbers in Urdu :

(1) واحد, Singular.

(2) جمع Plural.

When a Noun denotes one thing, it is called واحد, Singular Number. When it denotes more than one it is called جمع Plural Number.

اسم خاص Proper Nouns being the names of some particular person, place or thing are always واحد, Singular.

اسم جمع Collective Nouns are واحد, Singular but according to rule their Plural is formed as فوج army, فوجیں armies, جماعت company, جماعتیں companies.

Rules for forming Plural from Singular.

(1) Masculine Nouns ending in 'ا' alif or 'ہ' he are changed into یاے مجہول 'ے' ye, as :

لڑکا boy	لڑکے boys
مرغا cock	مرغے cocks
گھوڑا horse	گھوڑے horses
مدرسہ school	مدرسے schools

پردہ curtain — پردے curtains

ہفتہ week — ہفتے weeks

درجہ class — درجے classes

etc., etc.

(2) Masculine Nouns not ending in 'ا' or 'ہ' their Singular and Plural are the same, as:

پتھر مارا struck stone — پتھر مارے struck stones.

آدمي گیا man went — آدمي گئے men went

موتی خریدا bought pearl — موتي خریدے bought pearls

(3) Feminine Nouns ending in یاے معروف long 'ی' 'ا' alif and نون غنہ nasal ں n̲ are added, as:

روٹي bread — روٹیاں breads

لڑکي girl — لڑکیاں girls

چھڑي stick — چھڑیاں sticks

ٹوپي cap — ٹوپیاں caps

گھڑي watch — گھڑیاں watches

etc., etc

(4) Feminine Nouns not ending in یاے معروف 'ی' long یاے مجھول 'ے' short and نون غنہ nasal ں n̲ is added, as:

عورت woman — عورتیں women

فوج army — فوجیں armies

میز table	میزیں tables
تدبیر plan	تدبیریں plans
دیوال wall	دیواریں walls
جان life	جانیں lives

etc., etc.

(5) Feminine Nouns ending in 'ا' or 'و' váo 'ء' همزہ hamza 'ے' یاے مجہول ye and نون غنہ nasal nun is added, as :

دوا medicine	دوائیں medicines
تمنا desire	تمنائیں desires
گھٹا cloud	گھٹائیں clouds

etc., etc.

(6) Some Plurals are formed like Persian, as : هزارها thousands, بارها many twelve times, تھانہ جات police stations, etc.

(7) The Plural of Persian and Arabic words which are in use in Urdu is formed according to the Persian and Arabic rules, as :

اسم noun	اسماء nouns
فعل action	افعال actions

حرف letter	حروف letters
طرف side	اطراف sides

etc., etc.

(8) English words spoken in Urdu, their plural is formed according to the Urdu rules, as ;

ایک بٹن one button	دس بٹن ten buttons
اچھا بیگ good bag	اچھے بیگ good bags
ٹوٹا لمپ broken lamp	ٹوٹے لمپ broken lamps

See Rule 2 above.

کمپنی company	کمپنیاں companies
چمنی chimney	چمنیاں chimneys

See Rule 3 above.

کونسل council	کونسلیں councils
مشین machine	مشینیں machines
بوتل bottle	بوتلیں bottles

See Rule 4 above

C.—حالت Case.

1—Definition and Kinds.

حالت **Case** is that form of the noun which shows its relation to some other word in the sentence.

Urdu Nouns have four Principal Cases :

(1) حالت فاعلی **Nominative Case.**

(2) حالت مفعولی **Objective Case.**

(3) حالت اضافی **Possessive Case.**

(4) حالت ندائیہ **Vocative Case.**

(1) حالت فاعلی The **Nominative** names the agent, or one who does something, as کتا بھونکا *Dog* barked. *Dog* is in the Nominative Case.

(2) حالت مفعولی The **Objective** denotes the *object*, or that to which something is done, a سوہن نے ایک چڑیا پکڑی Sohan caught a *bird*. *Bird* is in the Objective Case.

(3) حالت اضافی The **Possessive** denotes the *possessor* or *owner*, as *Rama's* book or The book *of Rama*. *Rama* is in the Possessive Case.

Nominative and Objective Cases have connection with the Verb, but Noun also can have connection with another noun. This connection is called اضافت Sign of Possessive Case. The signs of Possessive case are کا-کی-کے 'of' or ('s) apostrophes, as موہن کا گھر The house *of* Mohan. Here Mohan has connection with the other noun *house*, therefore the noun Mohan having connection is called مضاف الیہ **Possessor,** and house with which he has connection is called مضاف **Possessed**

(4) The **Vocative** is used in calling, as اے بھائی میرے پاس آؤ O Brother come to me, and the Noun in the Vocative is called منادی **Nominative of Address.** Here *Brother* has been called and is in the Vocative Case and also Nominative of Address.

2.—حالتوں کی علامت اور اسم کی تبدیلیاں
Signs of Cases and Changes in Nouns.

(1) Signs.

(1) When a noun is the Nominative of an Intransitive Verb no change takes place in its form, as راما بیٹھا Rama sat.

(2) When a noun is the Nominative of a Transitive Verb and its tense is Past Indefinite, Present Perfect, Past Perfect, Doubtful Past نے the sign of Nominative is used, as رام نے سبق پڑھا Ram read the lesson. سوداگر نے ایک گھوڑا بیچا ہے The merchant has sold a horse, جواہر نے ایک گائے بیچی تھی Jawahir had sold a cow. عورتوں نے غلہ پیسا ہوگا The women might have ground the corn.

(3) No sign of Nominative 'نے' ne is used when a Verb is derived from the Transitive Root پھولنا ۔ بولنا ۔ لانا and with which Transitive Verbs the words لگنا یا سکنا ۔ چکنا ۔ جانا come, as لچھمن یہہ خبر لایا Lachhman brought this news. سب لڑکے سبق بھول گئے All boys forgot their lessons. سوداگر گھوڑا بیچنے لگا The merchant began to sell the horse.

(4) Like the sign "نے" ne of the Nominative of Transitive Verb, 'کو' to is the sign of Objective, as هیرا نے روهن کو مارا Hira struck Rohan, میں نے دس روپیہ بلونت کو دئے I gave ten rupees to Balwant.

(5) اضافت کی علامت sign of Possessive 'کا' is used when مضاف (Possessed) is Singular Masculine. 'کے' is used when مضاف (Possessed) is Plural Masculine and 'کی' when مضاف is Feminine, as درگا پرشاد کی گھوڑی ، سوهن کے لڑکے ، کرشنا کا گھوڑا.

(6) In Urdu مضاف الیہ Possessor comes first, next the اضافت (sign of Possessive Case) and then مضاف (Possessed), but in Persian مضاف (Possessed) first, then مضاف الیہ (Possessor) with a Vowel (ـِ) زیر the

sign of اضافت with the Possessed, as صاحب خانہ – گھر کا مالک Master of the house, دل انسان - انسان کا دل Heart of man.

(7) The sign of Vocative is حرف ندا Interjection which comes before the noun, as اے خدا ہم پر رحم کر O God have mercy upon us! 'اے' is the sign of Vocative, خدا is in the Vocative Case and منادی Nominative of Address. Sometimes 'اے' حرف ندا is dropped sa لڑکو - چپ چاپ بیٹھو Boys, sit quietly.

(2) Changes.

(1) When there is 'ا' or 'ہ' at the end of اسم واحد Singular Noun and signs of فاعل Nominative or مفعول Objective or Possessive or Vocative come, the 'ا' alif or 'ہ' are changed into 'ے' اے مجہول as لڑکے نے روٹی کھائی The boy ate the bread, میں نے اُستاد کو روپئے دئے I gave two rupees to the teacher, لڑکے کی کتاب کھو گئی The boy's book is lost. اے آدمی O man!

(2) When a Plural Noun is اسم فاعل Nominative or مفعول Objective or مضاف الیہ Possessive the Plural is changed into 'و' مجہول and 'ں' غنہ before the

signs of Nominative or Objective or Possessive, as لڑکوں نے سبق پڑھا The boys read the lesson. لچھمن نے چوھوں کو پکڑا Lachhman caught the mice لڑکوں کي کتابیں ختم ھوچکی ھیں The books of the boys are finished. بکریوں کا رنگ کالا ھے The colour the goats is black. لڑکوں نے گھوڑوں کو دیکھا The boys saw the horses.

(3) The nouns whose form of Singular and Plural is the same and are the Nominative or Objective or Possessive Case مجہول 'و' and غنہ 'ں' is added before their signs, as سپاھیون نے چوروں کو پکڑا The soldiers caught the thieves. چوروں نے مہاجن کو لوٹا The thieves robbed the banker. انھوں نے موروں کو مارا They shot the peacocks.

(4) In the Vocative Case the sign of plural of the noun is changed into مجہول 'و' as اے لڑکو O boys, اے لڑکیو O girls etc.

(5) In the Vocative Case of the nouns having their singular and plural forms the same واؤ مجہول is added at their end, as اے سوداگرو O merchants, اے لوگو O people.

D.—تصغیر—Diminutives

The name of a small thing in comparison with a large one is called تصغیر Diminutive.

(1) The lifeless objects which have no real جنس Gender are said to be مونث تصغیر Feminine Diminutive, as :

شیشہ shíshá	شیشی shíshí
پنکھا pankhá	پنکھی pankhí
ٹوکرا ṭokrá	ٹوکری ṭokrí
تھال thál	تھالی thálí

etc., etc.

(2) By adding one of یا - لی - لا - ڑی - - ڑا - ک at the end of a noun تصغیر Diminutive is formed, as :

ڈبا ḍibbá	ڈبیا ḍibiyá
کونڈا koṇḍá	کونڈالی koṇḍálí
کھاٹ kháṭ	کھٹولا khaṭolá
ٹانگ ṭáng	ٹنگڑی ṭangrí
مکھہ mukh	مکھڑا mukhṛá
ڈھول ḍhol	ڈھولک ḍholak

(3) In Persian تصغیر Diminutive is formed by adding ' چہ ' and 'یربہ' at the end. It is used in Urdu also, as :

باغ bág	باغچه bágcha
دیگ deg	دیگچه degcha
مشک mashk	مشکیزه mashkiza

etc., etc.

STUDY OF WORDS.

LESSON 1.

پتھر - سنگ stone	راے opinion
شارہ عام highway	سوال question
امیر البحر admiral	اجنبي stranger
جنگ battle	شہنشاہ emperor
زندگي life	خطوط letters
شہزادہ prince	نصیحت instructions
علم الہی theology	حاکم ruler
شہید martyr	رسومات rites
عمارت building	ماھیگیر fisher
نانبائی baker	کتبخانہ library
ملک country	مجرم culprit
زرگر goldsmith	چوپایہ quadruped
ابر cloud	عجائب گھر museum
چڑیا خانہ menagerie	رضا consent
فتح victory	شکست defeat
عدالت court	انبوہ crowd

حسن beauty
قیدی prisoner
شیرینی sweetness
تلخي bitterness
ترشي sourness
اصول policy
ایمانداري honesty
صبر patience
استقلال perseverance
کوه mountain
فرمانبرداری obedience
راستبازي righteousness
بادشاهت kingdom
بهشت heaven
دوزخ hell
عبادت worship
مذهب religion
مفلسی poverty
گناه sin
دولت wealth
کامیابی success
امتحان examination
محرر clerk
اطلاع information
مشق exercise
عادت habit

LESSON 2.

جانداروں کے جسم کے اعضا

Limbs of body of living beings.

سر head
رخسار cheek
پیشاني forehead
زنخ chin
کهوپڑي skull
کوا uvula
گوش ear
چشم eye
بال - مو hair
بلغم phlegm

بینی nose

شکم belly

چھاتي - سینه breast

پھیپھڑا lungs

گرده kidney

کہني elbow

مژگان eye-brow

دھانا mouth

مغض brain

جگر liver

کمر waist

کف - ھتھیلي palm

خایه testicles

زانو knee

پا foot

ناف navel

مونچھه mustache

انگشت پا toes

گوشت flesh

گلا - گلو throat

چہره face

زبان tongue

دندان tooth

دست hand

انگشت finger

نتھنے nostrils

دل heart

معده stomach

آنتیں intestines

دوش - کندھا shoulder

مشت fist

رحم womb

ایڑي heel

پسینا sweat

پشت back

ڈاڑھي beard

انگشت thumb

خون - لہو blood

LESSON 3.

حیوانات و چوپاے
Beasts and Quadrupeds

شیر lion	سگ dog
پلنگ - چیتا tiger	گاؤ cow
گاؤنر ox	میش - بھیڑ sheep
تیندوا leopard	بھیڑیا wolf
بھالو - ریچھ bear	گینڈا rhinoceros
شتر camel	خچر mule
بز - بکری goat	گلہری squirrel
بوزنہ - بندر monkey	ساهي porcupine
سیار - گیدڑ jackal	نیولا mungoose
خرگوش hare	برہ - ممیا lamb
حلوان kid	سم - گھر hoof
سمبور fur	دم tail
هاتھي elephant	چھچھوندر - کورموش mole
بھینس buffalo	لومڑی fox

پتنگے Insects

تتلي butterfly	شہد کی مکھی bee
بر wasp	جگنو firefly
جھینگر cricket	تڈا grass-hopper
تڈي locust	مچھر mosquito

بھنورا humble-bee	مکھی fly
بھنگا gnat	ڈانس gadfly.

کیڑے مکوڑے Worms.

چیونٹی ant	گبریلا beetle
جونک leech	کھٹمل bug
مکڑي spider	لیک nit
جوئیں louce	دیمک white-ant

LESSON 4.

پرندے Birds.

طوطا parrot	کبوتر pigeon
بلبل nightingale	فاختہ dove
بگلا heron	سارس crane
مرغا cock	مرغی hen
چمگادڑ bat	کوا crow
ڈوم کوا rook, raven	بط duck
گدھ vulture	چیل kite
ماهي خور king-fisher	هڑگیلا adjutant
الو owl	کٹھ پھوڑا woodpecker
مور peacock	مورنی peahen
گورا sparrow	ابابیل swallow
هنس goose	پیرو turkey

آبی اور رینگنے والے جانور

Aquatic animals and Reptiles.

مچھلی fish	مینڈھک frog
گرگٹان chameleon	بچھو-کژدم scorpion
گھونگھا snail	سانپ-مار snake, serpent
چھپکلی lizard	کیکڑا crab
جھینگا lobster	مگر crocodile
کالاسانپ cobra	سنکھ conch
کینچوا earthworm	گھڑیال-ناکہ alligator
کچھوا tortoise	سیپ oyster
گوجر - کانتر centepede	گوہ iguana

LESSON 5.

غلہ Cornseeds.

گیہوں wheat	چاول rice
جئی barley	دھان paddy
سابودانہ sago	چنا gram
دال pulse	مٹر peas
مکا maize	رینڈی castor-seed
السي linseed	تل sesame
پوستہ کا دانا poppy-seed	راي mustard-seed

پهل - میوہ Fruits

ام - انبہ mango	امرود guava
جامن blackberry	نورنگی-سنترہ orange
سیب apple	کهجور date
کیلا plantain	آڑهو peach
ناشپاتی pears	بیر plum
پهوٹ melon	نیبو lemon
خربوزہ-خرپزہ muskmelon	تربوز water-melon
پپیتا papaya	ناریل coconut
بادام almond	ککڑی cucumber
انگور grape	پستا Pistachio
اخروٹ walnut	کشمش resin
انجیر fig	املی tamarind
انار pomegranate	تاڑ palm
اناناس pine-apple	آمرا sourball
زیتون olive	شریفا custard-apple

پهول Flowers.

گلاب rose	نیلوفر lily
گیندا marygold	چمبیلی jessamine
کمل lotus	عشق پیچا ivy

ترکاریاں Vegetables.

گانٹهہ گوبی cabbage	پهول گوبهی cauliflower

بیگن brinjal	اروی arum
لہسن garlic	پیاز onion
آلو potato	رتالو yam
شکرقند sweet-potato	چقندر beet-root
لوکي pumpkin	مولی radish

LESSON 6.

اشیاے خوردنی

Eatables and foodstuffs.

روٹی bread	بھات rice
سالن curry	دودھ milk
مٹھا butter-milk	شکر - چینی sugar
گڑ jaggery	کھیر frumenty
پاؤروٹی loaf	مصری sugar-candy
دھی sour-milk	مٹھائی sweetmeats
مربا preserve	گوشت flesh
گوشت پکا meat	شوربا soup
بالائی cream	اچار pickle
ھرن کا گوشت venison	شہد honey
کباب roast	گھی clarified-butter

مصالحجات Spices

دھنیا coriander seed	کالی مرچ black-pepper
ھلدی turmeric	ادرک ginger

سونٹھ dry ginger	لال مرچ chillies
الایچی cardamum	لونگ cloves
دارچینی cinnamon	جاوتري mace
جایفل nutmeg	سونف aniseed
زیرہ cummin-seed	کتھا catechu
زعفران saffron	سپاري betelnut
کباب چیني cubeb	مشك musk
کافور camphor	تیج پتا cassia-leaf

LESSON 7.

لباس اور زیورات

Wearing Apparels.

زیورات ornaments	کڑا - چوڑی bangle
بالی ear-ring	کنگن - جوشن bracelet
کرتا coat	پاجامہ trousers
انگوٹھی ring	سلے کپڑے clothes
ھار necklace	قمیض shirt
جیب pocket	چدر sheet
تولیا towel	چغا cloak
ٹوپی دیسي cap	ٹوپي انگریزي hat
دستانے gloves	انگوچھا napkin

گھانگرا : سایہ gown
پگڑي - سافا turban
رومال handkerchief
پتلون pantaloon
موزے - پاتابہ stockings
استین sleeve
کمربند belt
چھینٹ chintz, prints
مخمل velvet
اون wool
ریشم silk
استر lining
فیتا tape
سوت - تاگا thread

اوزار و ھتھیار

Tools and weapons.

چاقو knife
قینچی scissors
بیلچا shovel
ھنسیا sickle
کلھاڑي hatchet
کدالی spade
آرا saw
ھل plough
سونٹا mace
برچھا - بھالا spear
تیر arrow
کمان bow
ڈھال - پھري shield
بندوق musket, rifle, gun
طپنچہ pistol, revolver
سنگین bayonet

مکان و سامان تعمیر وغیرہ

House and building materials etc.

عمارت edifice
محل palace
گھر-مکان house
کمرہ - کوٹھری room

بهوس کا گهر thatched house
اوسارا - سایه‌بان shed
گرجاگهر church
سراے inn
اتشدان fire-place
خوابگاه bedroom
اصطبل stable
کوٹها - بالا خانه balcony
برآمده verandah
دروازه door
دیوار wall
تهونی post
فرش floor
کاٹهه کی سیڑهی ladder
اینٹ brick
روڑا brick-bats
چونا lime
کڑي - دهرنی rafter
کهڑکی window
تخته plank
پینچ screw

مندر temple
جهوپڑي hut, cottage
مسجد mosque
گودام godown
باورچي خانه kitchen
غسل خانه bathroom
پاخانه latrine
بیٹهك خانه parlour
باغ garden
پهاٹك gate
بنیاد - نیو foundation
کهمبا pillar
چهت roof
سیڑهی - زینا stairs
گنبد arch, vault
کهپرا tile
بالو sand
شهتیر beam
چوکهٹ door-case
جهلمل blinds
کیل nail
چٹکنی latch

چھڑ - بیڑا bar	تالا lock
کنجی key	زنجیر chain

LESSON 8.

سامان خانگي (گرهستی)

Household Furniture.

پلنگ bedstead	الماري almirah
صندوق chest	لوہے کا صندوق iron-chest
میز table	کرسي chair
تپای stool	سیج couch
چٹائي mat	بستر bed
گھڑا pitcher	سراھي goblet
بالٹی - ڈول bucket	طباق plate
کٹوری - پیالہ bowl, cup	تھالي dish
کڑھاو caldron	رزائی quilt
تکیہ pillow	پردہ curtain
پلنگ کی چدر bedsheet	غالیچہ carpet
کمبل blanket	لالٹین lantern
مٹي کے برتن earthenware	چیني کے برتن chinaware
مرتبان jar	گھڑا - مٹکا water-pot
کڑاھی frying-pan	کیتلي kettle

اشیاء معدنی (کانی)
Minerals.

دھات - فلزات metal	جواہر jewel
سونا - زر gold	ھیرا diamond
سیم - چاندی silver	پھٹکری alum
اسپات steel	سوھاگا borax
کھان mine	نیلا توتھا blue vitriol
ھیراکسیس green vitriol	پیتل - پرنج brass
سیندور-شنگرف vermilion	تانبا copper
ابر کھڑ - بھوڑل talc, mica	جستا zinc
گندھک sulphur	رانگا leaf-tin
سیسا lead	مونگ coral
کانسا bell-metal	سنگ چقمق flint
لعل ruby	پتھر کا کوئلا coal, coke
زمرد emerald	موتي pearl
سنگ مرمر marble	کھڑیا متي chalk

سیندھالنمك rock-salt

LESSON 9.

اصطلاحات آئینی و عدالتي
Law and Court Technical Words.

عدالت court	قانون - شرع law
ثالث arbitrator	مدعي plaintiff

مدعا علیه defendant
مختار power-of-attorney
عرضي plaint
امر تنقیح طلب issue
گواه witness
گواهي با حلف deposition
تمسك bond
طلبي نامه - حکم حاضري summons
مچلکه security
بریت acquittal
قرقي attachment
سماعت hearing
نیلام auction
قید imprisonment
پهانسی hanging
جرمانه fine
قید خانه prison
حاجت - حوالات lock-up
هتکڑی handcuffs
دیوانی civil

وکیل pleader
مقدمه suit
دعوی claim
ثبوت - شهادت evidence
نالش complaint
پٹا lease
حلف oath
پروانه گرفتاري warrant
ضامن bail
فیصله decision
نظر ثاني revision
دستاویز document
امین bailiff
سزا punishment
موت کا capital
جلا وطنی به عبور دریائے شور
کالا پاني transportation
جیل خانه jail
بیڑی fetters
تهانه police-station
فوجداری criminal

خطا offence	جرم crime
مجرم guilty	ملزم accused
قتل murder	حرکت خلاف خیر خواهي بادشاه treason
خود کشي suicide	
چوري theft	زنا کاري adultery
جعل forgery	دروغ حلفي perjury
ازالہ حیثیت عرفی libel	گالی abuse
جوا gambling	رشوت bribe
ڈکیتي robbery	هنگامہ rioting
مداخلت مستلزم سزا trespass	ضرب hurt
ضرب شدید grievous hurt	بادشاہ کش یا کُشي regicide
پدر کُش یا کُشي patricide	مادر کُش یا کُشي matricide
برادر کُش کُشي fratricide	بچہ کُش یا کُشي infanticide

تحقیر عدالت contempt of court

LESSON 10.

وقت و دن Time and Days.

دن day	رات night
دوپہر noon	صبح morning
شام evening	تیسرا پہر afternoon

گهنٹہ hour	گهڑي moment
پل second	هفته week
آج to-day	کل to-morrow
آدهي رات mid-night	سال year
ماه - مهينه month	سن era
گذرا کل yesterday	شنبه Saturday
يك شنبه Sunday	سوموار - دوشنبه Monday
سه شنبه Tuesday	چهار شنبه Wednesday
پنجشنبه Thursday	جمعه Friday

صدی Century

رشته ناته Relatives.

والدين parents	والد father
مادر mother	برادر brother
همشيره sister	شوهر - خاوند husband
ابن - بيٹا - پسر son	دختر - بيٹی daughter
سوتيلا بيٹا step-son	سوتيلی بيٹي step-daughter
سوت co-wife	دادا - نانا grandfather
دادی-ناني grandmother	بهانجا - بهتيجا nephew
بهانجي-بهتيجي niece	چاچا- خالو - پهوپها - ماموں
چچي-خالا-پهوپهي-مماني	uncle
aunt	خسر father-in-law

خوش دامن mother-in-law سالا-بهنوئی-نندوئی brother-in-law

سالی - نند - بهاوج sister-in-law داماد son-in-law

بہو daughter-in-law

CHAPTER V.

II.—صفت THE ADJECTIVE.

A.—Definition and Kinds.

صفت **Adjective** is a qualifying word and it comes before a noun and after as well, as وہ طاقتور آدمی ہے He is a strong man. وہ آدمی طاقتور ہے That man is strong.

Adjective qualifies a Pronoun also and is Placed just after the Pronoun, as وہ ہوشیار نہیں ہے He is not clever. میں پیاسا ہوں I am thirsty.

Adjectives may be divided into five Principal classes :—

(1) صفت ذاتی Adjective of Quality.

(2) صفت مقداري Adjective of Quantity.

(3) صفت توصیفی Proper Adjective.

(4) صفت تعدادي Numeral Adjective.

(5) صفت اشارہ Demonstrative Adjective.

1.—صفت ذاتی **Adjectives of Quality** show the quality or state of the thing named, as موٹا آدمی a *fat* man, ھوشیار لڑکا a *clever* boy etc.

Some **Adjectives of Quality**—نیك - اچھا good, بد bad, چھوٹا small, بڑا large, نیچ low, سیاہ black, سرخ red, سخت hard. سفید white, نیا new, پرانا old, چوڑا wide, etc.

2.—صفت مقداری **Adjectives of Quantity** show how much of a thing is meant, as سیر بھر دودہ *a seer* of milk, گز بھر رسا *one yard* of rope, ایك من غلہ *one maund* of corn, زیادہ درد *much* pain, کچھہ دودہ *some* milk چھوٹا لڑکا *little* boy, etc.

3.—صفت نسبتی **Proper Adjectives** are formed from Proper Nouns, as ترکي ٹوپي *Turkish* cap, هندوستانی عورت *Indian* woman, انگریزی کتابیں *English* books. جرمنی کي چاندي *German* silver, چاپانی زبان *Japanese* language, etc.

4.—صفت تعدادي **Numeral Adjectives** say something about the number of a thing, as میں نے چار آدمی دیکھے I saw *four* men مجھے آٹھہ روپئے دو Give me *eight* rupees, ایك one, دس ten, سو hundred, ھزار thousand, etc.

Numeral Adjectives are of three kinds :—

(1) صفت عدد Definite Numeral Adjective.

(2) صفت مبہم Indefinite Numeral Adjective.

(3) صفت انفرادي Distributive Numeral Adjective.

(1) صفت عدد Definite Numeral Adjective denotes exact numbers.

They are divided into three kinds :—

(i) عدد **Cardinal Numeral** denotes *how many* as دس ten, چار four, etc.

(ii) صفت عددي **Ordinal Numeral** denotes order in series, as پہلا first, پانچواں fifth, etc.

(iii) صفت تضعیفی **Multiplicatives** show how often a thing is repeated, as سہ چند *three-fold*, دگنا *double* تہرا *triple*, etc.

(2) صفت مبہم Indefinite Numeral Adjectives do not denote any exact number, as سب *all*, کوئی *any*, چند *few*, بہت *many*, زیادہ *much*, بہت زیادہ *more*, نہایت - سب سے زیادہ *most*, etc.

(3) صفت انفرادي Distributive Numeral Adjectives denote that things are taken one at a time. They are فی - ایك ایك *each*, ہر ایك - ہرکس *every*, etc.

5.—صفت اشارہ **Demonstrative Adjectives** point out something, as اِس - یہہ *this* table, اُس - وہ *that* chair etc.

B.—صفت بنانے کے قاعدے

Rules for the formation of Adjectives

(1) Some صفت Adjectives are formed without any rule. They are originally so, as اچھا good, کالا black, ہرا green, تھوڑا little, etc.

(2) Some صفت ذاتي Adjectives of Quality are formed by adding 'الف' to a noun, as ٹھنڈا cool from ٹھنڈ cold, میلا dirty, میل dirt, etc.

Sometimes صفت ذاتی is formed by joining two nouns, as انمول invaluable, نڈر fearless, من چلا whimsical, بے ڈول ugly, deformed.

Some Persian Adjectives are also used in Urdu, as ایک good, بد bad, بہادر brave, etc.

Some Arabic Adjectives are also used in Urdu, as امیر rich, غریب. poor, شجاع brave, احمق stupid, etc.

(3) There is no rule for forming صفت مقداري Adjective of Quantity.

(4) صفت نسبتي Proper Adjectives are formed by adding یاے معروف 'ي' to the noun, as مدراسی

Madrasee from مدراس Madras, چيني Chinese from چين China, etc.

Nouns ending in 'ی' or 'ہ' drop 'ی' and 'ہ' and add وی wí to the noun, as دهلوي of Delhi from دهلی Delhi, بريلوی of Bareilly from بريلي Bareilly.

Sometimes 'ہ' is dropped and 'ي' is added, as بنگالي from بنگلہ

Sometimes Proper adjective is formed by adding آنی ání to the Persian words, as جسمانی bodily from جسم body, روحانی spiritual from روح spirit.

(5) Numbers 1, 2, 3, 4, etc., etc. are taken in Urdu from Hindi.

When by any number all the things are meant واو مجهول 'و' and نون غنہ 'ں' is added after it, as چاروں لڑکے پاس هو گئے All the four boys passed the examination, دونوں بهائي Both brothers, etc.

صفت عددي Ordinal Numeral is formed by adding واں wán at the end of the number, as آٹهواں eighth, دسواں tenth, etc., but دوسرا – تيسرا – چوتها – چهٹا are not formed according to this rule.

When an Ordinal Numeral is formed from a compound number واں wán is added to the last number, as ایکسو ساتواں ek sau sátwán (hundred and seventh, 107th) ایکسو بیسواں (hundred and twentieth, 120th).

Persian Ordinal Numeral used in Urdu, as اول لڑکا auwal laṛká (first boy), چہارم جماعت chahárum jamá'at (fourth class).

صفت تضعيفي Multiplicatives are formed by adding گنا guná after the number, as پانچ گنا fivefold, چھہ گنا sixfold, دو گنا double, تین گنا triple, etc.

Persian صفت تضعیفی Multiplicatives are also used in Urdu, as دوچند double, twofold, سہ چند threefold, triple, etc.

There are some settled words for Indefinite Numeral Adjective. They are کئی several, کوئی any, بہت many, چند few, بعضے some, etc.

C.— صفت کي گردان

Inflection of Adjectives.

No change takes place in English and Persian Adjectives to show the Gender and Number, but in Urdu it does.

(1) صفت ذاتی Adjective of Quality and صفت مقداری Adjective of Quantity ending in 'الف' the 'الف' alifs are changed into 'ي' یاے مجہول and for feminine into یاے معروف, as اچھا لڑکا good boy, اچھے لڑکے good boys, اچھی لڑکی good girl, اچھی لڑکیاں good girls, etc.

To show the quality or state Urdu Adjective is also changed with the موصوف (thing qualified), as اچھا لڑکا اپنا سبق یاد کرتاھے Good boy learns his lesson, اچھےلڑکے خوب بڑھتے ھیں Good boys learn well, etc.

When the موصوف (thing qualified) is such a noun which has no change in Singular and Plural the Urdu Adjective, owing to the number is changed, as چھت سے ایک بڑا سانپ گرا A large snake fell from the roof گڈھے میں سے بڑے سانپ نکلے Large snakes came out of the pit.

But the Arabic and Persian Adjectives used in Urdu never change, as یہہ عمدہ چھڑي ھے This is a good stick. یے عمدہ گھڑیاں ھیں These are good clocks. وہ سرخ گھوڑے کو لایا He brought the red horse. یے سرخ گھوڑے میرے ھیں These red horses are mine.

D.—صفت کے درجے

Degrees of Comparison.

صفت Adjectives have three **Degrees of Comparison** :—

(1) تفضیل نفسی **Positive Degree.**

(2) تفضیل بعض **Comparative Degree.**

(3) تفضیل کل **Superlative Degree.**

(1) The تفضیل نفسی **Positive** expresses the simple quality, as نیک good, مہربان kind. بڑا large, etc.

(2) تفضیل بعض **Comparative** expresses the higher or lower degree of the quality, as زیادہ یا بہت مہربان kinder, زیادہ یا بہت بڑا larger, etc.

تفضیل بعض The Comparative is used when two objects are compared, as موهن لچهمن سے زیادہ مہربان هے Mohan is *kinder* than Lachman.

(3) تفضیل کل **Superlative** expresses the highest or lowest degree, as سب سے زیادہ یا بہت هي مہربان kindest, سب سے زیادہ یا بہت هی بڑا largest, etc.

تفضیل کل **Superlative** is used when more than two objects are compared, as موهن سب سے زیادہ یا بہت هی مہر بان هے Mohan is *kindest* of all.

In Persian تفضيل بعض Comparative and تفضيل كل Superlative Degrees are formed by adding ' تر ' and ' ترين ' to the تفضيل نفسي Positive, as نيك good نيك تر better, نيك ترين best, etc.

تفضيل بعض and تفضيل كل of the Persian Adjectives used in Urdu are formed in the Persian way, as به good, بهتر better, بهترين best ; بد bad, بدتر worse, بدترين worst, etc.

STUDY OF WORDS

LESSON 1.

بھاری heavy	خوش glad
موٹا fat	چپٹا flat
گول round	پاک holy
خشک dry	پتلا thin
زیادہ more	کم less
سب سے زیادہ most	سب سے کم least
مفید useful	چھوٹا small
عمیق گہرا deep	اندھا blind
دور far	سونہلا golden
نہایت extreme	کامل perfect
خالی empty	مردہ dead

کم خوبصورت less beautiful	نزدیک near
محنتی diligent	لنگڑا lame
طاقتور strong	خالص pure
قیمتی - بیش قیمت precious	غلط wrong
صحیح right	رنجیدہ sad
بالغ major	نابالغ minor
ناخوش unhappy	خوبصورت beautiful
عمدہ fine	نیچے درجہ کا inferior
عجیب - حیرت خیز wonderful	چھوٹا (عہدہ یا عمر میں) junior
بڑا (عمر یا عہدہ میں) senior	خراب - بد - برا bad, evil, ill
زیادہ دور farther	پرانا - بڈھا old
قابل able	صاف clean
جاری current	بے رحم cruel
نازک delicate	تربیت پذیر docile
بلند high	خوش اسلوب elegant
خوش گفتار - لسان eloquent	ایماندار honest
خوشبودار fragrant	فیاض generous
عاجز humble	پیچیدہ intricate

شریف noble

ضدی obstinate

خوش خلق - خلیق polite

متوجه attentive

هوادار airy

هنرمند artful

برادرانه brotherly

بزدل coward

ناقص defective

منحصر dependent

قابل تقسیم divisible

مشکوك doubtful

حاسد envious

قابل عذر objectionable

خوب excellent

مهلك fatal

پدرانه fatherly

خوفناك fearful

بناوتی fictitious

دوستانه friendly

پهلدار fruitful

جلالی glorious

بسیار خور gluttonous

گهاس‌دار grassy

عادی habitual

بهادرانه heroic

LESSON 2.

۱	ایك	1 one
۲	دو	2 two
۳	تین	3 three
۴	چار	4 four
۵	پانچ	5 five
۶	چهه	6 six
۷	سات	7 seven
۸	آٹهه	8 eight
۹	نو	9 nine
۱۰	دس	10 ten
۱۱	گیاره	11 eleven
۱۲	باره	12 twelve
۱۳	تیره	13 thirteen
۱۴	چوده	14 fourteen

۱۵ پندرہ 15 fifteen
۱۶ سولہ 16 sixteen
۱۷ سترہ 17 seventeen
۱۸ اٹھارہ 18 eighteen
۱۹ اُنیس 19 nineteen
۲۰ بیس 20 twenty
۲۱ اکیس 21 twenty-one
۲۲ بائیس 22 twenty-two
۲۳ تیئس 23 twenty-three
۲۴ چوبیس 24 twenty-four
۲۵ پچیس 25 twenty-five
۲۶ چھبیس 26 twenty-six
۲۷ ستائیس 27 twenty-seven
۲۸ اٹھائیس 28 twenty-eight
۲۹ اُنتیس 29 twenty-nine
۳۰ تیس 30 thirty
۳۱ اکتیس 31 thirty-one
۳۲ بتیس 32 thiry-two
۳۳ تینتس 33 thirty-three
۳۴ چونتیس 44 thirty-four
۳۵ پینتیس 35 thirty-five
۳۶ چھتیس 36 thirty-six
۳۷ سینتیس 37 thirty-seven
۳۸ ارتیس 38 thirty-eight
۳۹ انتالیس 39 thirty-nine
۴۰ چالیس 40 forty
۴۱ اکتالیس 41 forty-one
۴۲ بیالس 42 forty-two
۴۳ تینتالیس 43 forty-three
۴۴ چوالیس 44 forty-four
۴۵ پینتالیس 45 forty-five
۴۶ چھیالیس 46 forty-six
۴۷ سینتالیس 47 forty-seven
۴۸ ازتالیس 48 forty-eight
۴۹ اُنچاس 49 forty-nine
۵۰ پچاس 50 fifty

۵۱ اکاون 51 fifty-one
۵۲ باون 52 fifty-two
۵۳ ترپن 53 fifty-three
۵۴ چون 54 fifty-four
۵۵ پچپن 55 fifty-five
۵۶ چھپن 56 fifty-six
۵۷ ستاون 57 fifty-seven
۵۸ اٹھاون 58 fifty-eight
۵۹ انسٹھ 59 fifty-nine
۶۰ ساٹھ 60 sixty
۶۱ اکسٹھ 61 sixty-one
۶۲ باسٹھ 62 sixty-two
۶۳ ترسٹھ 63 sixty-three
۶۴ چوسٹھ 64 sixty-four
۶۵ پینسٹھ 65 sixty-five
۶۶ چھیاسٹھ 66 sixty-six
۶۷ سڑسٹھ 67 sixty-seven
۶۸ اڑسٹھ 68 sixty-eight
۶۹ انہتر 69 sixty-nine
۷۰ سٹر 70 seventy
۷۱ اکہتر 71 seventy-one
۷۲ بہتر 72 seventy-two
۷۳ تہتر 73 seventy-three
۷۴ چوہتر 74 seventy-four
۷۵ پچہتر 75 seventy-five
۷۶ چھیتر 76 seventy-six
۷۷ ستتر 77 seventy-seven
۷۸ اٹھتر 78 seventy-eight
۷۹ اناسي 79 seventy-nine
۸۰ اسی 80 eighty
۸۱ اکیاسی 81 eighty-one
۸۲ بیاسی 82 eighty-two
۸۳ تراسي 83 eighty-three
۸۴ چوراسی 84 eighty-four
۸۵ پچاسی 85 eighty-five
۸۶ چھیاسی 86 eighty-six
۸۷ ستاسي 87 eighty-seven
۸۸ اٹھاسي 88 eighty-eight
۸۹ نواسی 89 eighty-nine
۹۰ نوے 90 ninety
۹۱ اکانوے 91 ninety-one
۹۲ بانوے 92 ninety-two

۹۳ ترانوے 93 ninety-three	۹۷ ستانوے 97 ninety-seven
۹۴ چورانوے 94 ninety-four	۹۸ اٹھانوے 98 ninety-eight
۹۵ پنچانوے 95 ninety-five	۹۹ ننانوے 99 ninety-nine
۹۶ چھیانوے 96 ninety-six	۱۰۰ سو 100 hundred

۱۰۱ ایک سو ایک one hundred and one

(*and so on*)

۱۰۰۰ ایک ہزار	1000 one thousand
۱۰۰۰۰۰ ایک لاکھ	100000 one lac
۱۰۰۰۰۰۰۰ ایک کروڑ	10000000 one crore

LESSON 4.

پہلا first	گیارھواں eleventh
دوسرا second	بارھواں twelfth
تیسرا third	تیرھواں thirteenth
چوتھا fourth	چودھواں fourteenth
پانچواں fifth	پندرھواں fifteenth
چھٹواں sixth	سولھواں sixteenth
ساتواں seventh	سترھواں seventeenth
آٹھواں eighth	اٹھارواں eighteenth
نواں ninth	اُنیسواں nineteenth
دسواں tenth	بیسواں twentieth

(*and so on*). Use واں after the number.

کسر Fraction.

¼	پاو	$\frac{1}{4}$ one-fourth
½	نصف - آدھا	$\frac{1}{2}$ half
¾	پون	$\frac{3}{4}$ three-fourths
1¼	سوا	$1\frac{1}{4}$ one+one-fourth
1½	ڈیڑھ	$1\frac{1}{2}$ one+half
1¾	پونے دو	$1\frac{3}{4}$ one+three-fourths

CHAPTER VI

III.—ضمیر The PRONOUN

A.—تعریف اور قسمیں Definition and Kinds

ضمیر The **Pronoun** is a word used in place of a Noun, as گووند یہاں نہیں ہے وہ کھیل کے میدان میں ہے Govind is not here ; *he* is in the play-ground. (Here وہ, *he* is used in place of Govind.)

The principal classes of Pronouns are :

(1) ضمیر شخصی **Personal Pronoun.**

(2) ضمیر اشارہ **Demonstrative Pronoun.**

(3) ضمیر موصول **Relative Pronoun.**

(4) ضمیر استفہام **Interrogative Pronoun**

(5) ضمیر مبہم **Indefinite Pronoun.**

1.—ضمیر شخصي Personal Pronouns.

ضمیر شخصي **Personal Pronouns** are so called because they stand for the person speaking, spoken to or spoken of.

There are three **persons** :—

(*i*) ضمیر متکلم **The First Person**, which denotes the person *speaking*, as میں I, هم We, etc.

(*ii*) ضمیر حاضر **The Second Person**, which denotes the person *spoken to*, as تو thou, تم you, etc.

(*iii*) ضمیرغایب **The Third Person**, which denotes the person or thing *spoken of*, as وه, he, she, it, etc.

B.—ضمیر شخصی کی گردان

Declension of Personal Pronouns.

ضمیر متکلم *1st Person* (مذکر *Masc. or* مونث *Fem.*)

		واحد *Singular*		جمع *Plural*
ضمیر فاعلي *Nom.*	میں	I	هم	We
ضمیر مضاف الہ *Poss.*	میرا	My or Mine	همارا	Our or Ours
ضمیر مفعول *Objective*	مجھے	Me	همیں	Us

ضمیر حاضر *2nd Person* (مذکر *Masc. or* مونث *Fem.*)

		واحد *Singular*		جمع *Plural*
ضمیر فاعلی	*Nom.*	تو Thou		تم Ye or You
ضمیر مضاف الیہ	*Poss.*	تیرا Thy or Thine		تمہارا Your or Yours
ضمیر مفعول	*Obj.*	تجھے Thee		تمہیں You

ضمیر غایب *3rd Person* مذکر *Masc.* مونث *Fem.*

ضمیر فاعلی	*Nom.*	وہ He	وہ She
ضمیر مضاف الیہ	*Poss.*	اُسکا His	اسکا Her or Hers
ضمیر مفعول	*Obj.*	اسے - اسکا Him	اسکا - اسے Her

بے جان *Neuter.* عام *All Genders*

ضمیر فاعلی	*Nom.*	وہ It	وے They
ضمیر مضاف الیہ	*Poss.*	اُسکا Its	اُنکا Their or Theirs
ضمیر مفعول	*Obj.*	اسکو اسے It	اُنہیں - اُنکو Them

C.—Some special Uses of ضمیر Pronoun.

(1) " میں I " is always used in Singular. By the way of humility ' کمترین ' – ' بندہ ' - ' تابعدار ' are often used.

(2) " ھم We, " though it is the plural of " میں " it is now-a-days mostly used in Singular. Newspaper Editors use ' ھم ' for themselves.

Therefore in plural sense the word 'لوگ' is generally used, as 'هم‌لوگ'

(3) "تو Thou" is used for God and inferior persons, as اے خدا تو میری حفاظت کر O God thou save me !

(4) "تم You" although it is the plural of "تو Thou" still people use it for common and younger persons, as رام لال تم بڑے خراب آدمی هو Ram Lal you are a very bad man.

(5) For the respectable persons "آپ" "جناب" "حضور" in Singular and "آپ لوگ" in Plural is used instead of "تم" "تم لوگ" as صاحبو آپ لوگوں کو جلسه میں ضرور آنا چاهئے Gentlemen you must come in the meeting.

(6) "وہ" is always used in Singular but in its plural 'وے' the word "لوگ" is added, as وے لوگ لڑائي پر جارهے هیں They are going on war.

(7) The plural of 'اُس' becomes اُنهوں when نے is used after them.

(8) When in a sentence two pronouns come, one ضمیر فاعل and the other ضمیر مضاف آلہ the 2nd pronoun is changed into 'اپنا' 'اپنے' or 'اپنی' as تو اپنا گھر سمبھال Thou manage thy home. 'ہم' اپنے گھر جائیں We go our homes. 'وہ' اپني کتاب پڑھتا ہے He reads his book.

2.—ضمیر اشارہ Demonstrative Pronouns.

There are four ضمیر اشارہ Demonstrative Pronouns.

یہہ This	وہ That
یے These	وے Those

(1) When 'یہہ' is followed by a case-ending یہہ is changed into 'اس', as 'اسنے' - 'اسکو' - 'اسمیں' -

(2) When 'نے' is added to 'یے' then 'ے' is changed into 'ان' as انہوں نے - ان سے - ان کا - ان پر etc.

(3) To show the certainty and emphasis for any thing 'ی' یاے مجہول is added to اس - یہہ and ان as آج اسي نے جلسہ میں گایا تھا - کل بہی یہاں تھا انہیں نے کہا تھا

3.—ضمیر موصول Relative Pronouns.

ضمیر موصول Relative Pronoun is so called because it relates, or refers, to موصول an **Antecedent** (A noun, a clause or a sentence coming after a Relative Pronoun is called its موصول *Antecedent*.)

The **Relative Pronouns** are :—

' جو ' - ' جس ' ' جونسا ' who, which, that and what. ' جو ' is used for Masculine or Feminine in singular or plural alike.

' جونسا ' is used for Singular Masculine. In plural ' الف ' is changed into ' یاے مجہول ', as جونسے and in Singular and Plural Feminine into ' یاے معروف ' as جونسي

' جس ' in plural is changed into جن and when 'نے' comes after جن—' جنھوں ' is used in place of جن -

4.—ضمیر استفہام Interrogative Pronoun.

ضمیر استفہام **Interrogative Pronouns** are used in asking questions.

They are کس - کون *who*, کونسے - کونسي - کونسا *which*, کیا *what*. ' کس ' and ' کون ' *who* is applied to persons in both Numbers and both Genders, as

کون آیا یا آئي Who came ? کس نے یہہ کیا Who did it ? یہہ کسکا چاقو هے Whose knife is this ? تم کسکو بلاتے هو Whom do you call ?

' کونسا ' - ' کونسی ' - ' کونسے ' *which* applies to persons as well as things, as تم کونسا لوگے Which will you have ? کونسي چھڑی مضبوط هے Which stick is strong ? کونسے صندوق خالي هیں Which boxes are empty ?

' کیا ' *what* is applied to things, as تم نے کیا پایا What did you get ?

5.—ضمیر مبهم Indefinite Pronouns.

Indefinite Pronouns do not mark out or point to any particular person or thing. Such words, as 'کوئي' someone, any, 'سب' all 'بعض' some, 'کئي' several 'کچھه' something are Indefinite Pronouns.

(1) ' کوئي ' *someone, any* is often used in Singular, as I have not got any book. By repeating it twice it is counted as plural, as کوئی کوئی ریل پر سفر کرنا پسند نهیں کرتے Some (people) don't like to travel on the Railway train. When it is followed by a case-ending it is changed into ' کسی ' as کسی نے - کسي کا - کسی کی

(2) To show the certainty of anything 'نہ کوئی' is added to 'کوئی', as کوئی نہ کوئی اسے لے گیا ہے Some one must have taken it away.

(3) 'کچھ' *some*, *something* has no plural. It is used in the sense of quantity and in Nominative and Objective Cases, as

Nominative.—کچھ شک ہوتا ہے I feel some doubt.

Objective.—چندرا نے کچھ کھایا ہے Chandra has eaten something.

(4) 'کئی' *several* is the plural of 'کوئی' as کئی کتابیں Several books, کئی لڑکے Several boys.

(5) 'بعض' *some* is used for both the animate or inanimate objects in both Genders, as بعض کہتے ہیں کہ زمین گول نہیں Some say that earth is not round, بعض لڑکے Some boys, بعض لڑکیاں Some girls.

STUDY OF WORDS.

(1)

(کئی میں سے ہر ایک ہر ایک (دو یا کئی میں سے ایک) each	every
دو میں سے ایک۔دونوں	either
دو میں سے ایک بھی نہیں neither	کئی several
کوئی۔فلانہ	certain

کچھہ۔کوئي۔ایك اد some	سب all
کوئی نہیں none	کوئي any
دوسرا other	کوئی دوسرا۔کوئی اور another
کون - جو - کس who	جسکا of whom
کون - جو what	کسکا - جسکا whose
کون۔جو۔جسے۔کس which	جو that

(2)

جو - جوکوئی - چاهے کوئی - جس کسی نے - کوئي هو who ever.

هر کوئی - جو کوئي - چاهے کوئی who ever.

چاهے یهه - چاهے وه - جونسا whichever.

چاهے یهه - چاهے وه - جونسا whichsoever.

جو کچهه - چاهے کیسے هي whatever.

جو کچهه - سب کچهه - جو چیز - جس طرحکا whatsoever

خود میں - آپ هي - اپنے کو myself.

هم خود - اپنے آپ - اپنے آپ کو ourselves.

خود تو - تو هي - اپنے اوپر thyself, himself.

اپنے تئیں - وے خود - خود انهوں نے themselves.

آپ خود - آپ هي کو - خود اپنے سے yourself.

خود آپ - اپنے تئیں himself, herself.

CHAPTER VII.

IV.—فعل The VERB.

1.—تعریف اور قسمیں Definition and Kinds.

فعل**A Verb** is a word which declares or asserts something. Most Verbs also express being or doing with sign of time or tense.

The Verb is the chief word in a sentence. There can be no sentence without a فعل Verb.

Verbs are divided into two classes:—

(1) فعل متعدي Transitive Verb.

(2) فعل لازمی Intransitive Verb.

(1) فعل متعدی Transitive Verb.

When an action passes from the *doer* to an object it is فعل متعدی **Transitive Verb,** as گوپال اپنے بھائي کو پیار کرتا ھے Gopal *loves* his brother. Here *loves* is Transitive Verb because *brother* is the object of *loves*.

فعل متعدي Transitive Verb has two وضع یا صورت **Voices:**

(i) صورت معروف Active Voice.

(ii) صورت مجہول Passive Voice.

(i) صورت معروف **The Active Voice** denotes that the فاعل Subject of a فعل Verb acts, as John *wrote* a letter.

(ii) صورت مجہول **The Passive Voice** denotes that the فعل Subject of a فعل Verb is acted upon, as ایك خط اُس سے لکھا گیا A letter *was written* by him.

(2) - فعل لازمي **Intransitive Verb.**

When an action stops with the doer and does not pass over to some object it is فعل لازمي **Intransitive Verb**, as پرند اُڑتے ہیں Birds fly, میں اُٹھا I got up.

2.—زمانہ **Tense.**

زمانہ **Tense** expresses the time of an action.

There are three great divisions of time :—

(1) ماضي **Past Tense.**

(2) حال **Present Tense.**

(3) مستقبل **Future Tense.**

(1) زمانہ ماضي The **Past Tense** denotes that the action took place, or was going on in time past, as کرامت آیا Karamat came, کرشنا نے روٹي کھائی Krishna ate bread, وہ جارہاتھا, He was going.

(2) زمانہ حال The **Present Tense** denotes that the action is going on now, as موہن آتا ہے Mohan comes, میں پیار کر رہا ہوں I an loving.

(3) زمانہ مستقبل The **Future Tense** denotes that the action is yet to take place, as میں جاؤنگا I shall go, وہ جائیگا He will go.

Sometimes it happens that حال Present and مستقبل Future Tenses are found in فعل Verb, as محمود روٹی کھائے Mahmúd may eat bread. In فعل Verb کھائے "may eat" Present and Future Tenses are found. Such فعل is called مضارع **Aorist**.

Some Verbs indicate command or instructions, as جاؤ go کھا eat, سو sleep. Such Verbs are called فعل امر **Imperative**.

Some Verbs indicate command with prohibition, as مت جاؤ Don't go ; نہ بولو Don't speak. Such Verbs are called فعل نہی **Negative Imperative**.

With the view of زمانہ **Tense** there are six kinds of فعل Verbs :—

(1) فعل ماضی **Past Tense**.

(2) فعل حال **Present Tense**.

(3) فعل مستقبل Future Tense.

(4) فعل مضارع Aorist.

(5) فعل امر Imperative.

(6) فعل نہی Negative Imperative.

8.—لازم فعلوں کی گردان

Conjugation of Intransitive Verbs.

(1) فعل ماضی Past Tense.

There are six forms of فعل ماضی Past Tense :—

(a) ماضی مطلق Past Indefinite Tense.
(b) ماضی قریب Present Perfect Tense.
(c) ماضی بعید Pluperfect or Past Tense.
(d) ماضی ناتمام Past Continuous or Past Imperfect Tense.
(e) ماضی شکیہ Doubtful Past Tense.
(f) ماضی تمنائی یا شرطیہ Conditional Past Tense.

(a)—ماضی مطلق Past Indefinite Tense.

ماضی مطلق Past Indefinite is used to express a single act in past time, as دوڑا ran, آیا came, کھایا ate, میں نے پیار کیا I *loved*, احمد گیا Ahmad *went*.

Rules for the formation of Past Indefinite Tense.

(*i*) It is formed by changing the sign 'نا' of مصدر Root into 'الف', as from دوڑنا run دوڑا ran, from کھانا eat کھایا ate, etc.

(*ii*) If after dropping نا there is 'الف' alif or 'واو', then یا is added in the last, as آیا came from آنا come, دھویا washed from دھونا wash.

(*iii*) ماضی مطلق The Past Indefinites of some مصدر Roots are not formed according to the above rules. They are called بے قاعدہ فعل **Irregular Verbs**

مصدر *Root*	ماضی مطلق *Past Indefinite*
جانا go	گیا went
ہونا be	ہوا was
کرنا do	کیا did
مرنا die	مرا - موا died

گردان **Conjugation** of ماضی مطلق Past Indefinite Tense :

مذکر *Masculine.*

	صیغہ متکلم *1st Person*	صیغہ حاضر *2nd Person*	صیغہ غائب *3rd Person*
واحد *Sing.*	میں آیا I came	توآیا Thou came	وہ آیا He came
جمع *Plur.*	ہم آئے We came	تم آئے You came	وے ائے They came

مونث *Feminine.*

واحد *Sing.*	میں آئی I came	تو آئی Thou came	وہ آئی She came
جمع *Plur.*	ہم آئیں We came	تم آئیں You came	وے آئیں They came

(*b*) ماضي قریب **Present Perfect Tense**

ماضی قریب The Present Perfect Tense denotes that the action has just now been completed, as میں نے کھانا کھایا ھے I have dined, آیا ھے has come, گیا ھے has gone, کھایا ھے has dined, etc.

The way of forming this Tense is :—

(*i*) Add 'ھوں' to فعل Verb in the ماضی مطلق Past Indefinite Tense in صیغہ واحد متکلم singular 1st Person ; in the جمع متکلم plural 'ھیں' and in the

صیغہ واحد حاضر اورغائب 2nd and 3rd Person singular 'ھے' and in جمع حاضر 2nd Person plural 'ھو' and in جمع غائب 3rd Person plural ھیں -

(ii) گردان **Conjugation** of ماضی قریب Present Perfect Tense.

مذکر *Masculine.*

	صیغہ متکلم	صیغہ حاضر	صیغہ غائب
	1st Person	*2nd Person*	*3rd Person*
واحد	میں آیا ھوں	تو آیا ھے	وہ آیا ھے
Sing.	I have come.	Thou hast come.	He has come
جمع	ھم آئے ھیں	تم آئے ھو	ے آئے ھیں
Plur.	We have come.	You have come.	They have come

مؤنث *Feminine.*

واحد	میں آئي ھوں	تو آئي ھے	وہ آئي ھے
جمع	ھم آئي ھیں	تم آئی ھو	وے آئي ھیں

(c)—ماضي بعید Past Perfect Tense.

ماضی بعید Past Perfect Tense denotes that at a certain past time an action was complete, as آیا تھا had come, گیاتھا had gone, سویا تھا had slept, رام داس نے دودہ پیا تھا Ram Das had drunk the milk, etc.

In forming the Verbs in this tense add تھا in Masculine and تھي in Feminine.

گردان **Conjugation** of Past Perfect Tense

Masculine.

	1st P.	*2nd P.*	*3rd P.*
Sing.	میں گیا تھا	تو گیا تھا	وہ گیا تھا
	I had gone.	Thou hadst gone.	He had gone
Plur.	هم گئے تھے	تم گئے تھے	وے گئے تھے
	We had gone.	You had gone.	They had gone.

Feminine.

Sing.	میں گئی تھی	تو گئی تھی	وہ گئي تھی
	I had gone.	Thou hadst gone.	She had gone.
Plur.	هم گئي تھیں	تم گئي تھیں	وے گئي تھیں
	We had gone.	You had gone.	They had gone.

(*d*)—ماضی ناتمام یا استمراري Past Imperfect Tense.

This Tense expresses an action which began in some past time but not finished میں جاتا تھا یا جارها تھا I was going.

In forming Verb of this Tense drop the sign of مصدر (نا) and add تاتھا or رهاتھا as جاتاتھا, کرتاتھا, آرها تھا, جا رها تھا, آتا تھا.

گردان Conjugation of Past Imperfect Tense

Masculine.

	Singular	*Plural*
1st P.	میں آتا تھا یا آرھا تھا	ھم آتے تھے یا آرھے تھے
	I was coming	We were coming
2nd P.	تو آتا تھا یا آرھا تھا	تم آتے تھے یا آرھے تھے
	Thou wast coming	You were coming
3rd P.	وہ آتا تھا یا آرھا تھا	وے آتے تھے یا آرھے تھے
	He was coming	They were coming

Feminine.

1st P.	میں آتي تھی یاآرھی تھی	ھمآتي تھیں یاآرھی تھیں
	I was coming	We were coming
2nd P.	تو آتيتھی یاآرھی تھي	تم آتی تھیں یاآرھی تھیں
	Thou wast coming	You were coming
3rd P.	وہ آتي تھیيآرھي تھي	وےآتي تھیں یا آرھي تھیں
	She was coming	They were coming

(e) ماضی شکیہ—Doubtful Past Tense.

ماضی‌شکیہ **Doubtful Past Tense** expresses doubt whether an action was done or not in the past time, as میں گیا ھوؤنگا I might have gone.

Doubt in the Past Tense is expressed by adding

ھونگا - ھوگا - ھوگے - ھونگے - ھوگي - ھونگی

گردان Conjugation of Doubtful Past Tense.

Masculine.

	Singular.	*Plural.*
1st Per.	میں گیا ہونگا	ہم گئے ہونگے
	I might have gone	We might have gone
2nd Per.	تو گیا ہوگا	تم گئے ہوگے
	Thou mightest have gone	You might have gone
3rd Per.	وہ گیا ہوگا	وے گئے ہونگے
	He might have gone	They might have gone

Feminine.

1st.	میں گئی ہوؤنگی	ہم گئي ہونگي
	I might have gone	We might have gone
2nd.	تو گئي ہوگي	تم گئي ہوگی
	Thou mightest have gone	You might have gone
3rd.	وہ گئي ہوگي	وے گئي ہونگي
	She might have gone	They might have gone

(*f*) ماضی تمنائي یا شرطیہ Conditional Past Tense.

ماضي تمنائي یا شرطیہ Conditional Past Tense is formed by adding ' تا ' to the root. It changes into تے and تی according to the Subject, a اگرمیں آتا If I had come. اگر ہم آتے If we had come. Conditional clause is always followed by 'تو' (then), as

تم کھاتے تو میں بھی تمہارے ساتھہ کھاتا If you had eaten (then) I too would have eaten with you. As تو has the full force of condition in a sentence اگر is often dropped.

(2) فعل حال Present Tense.

There are four forms of the فعل حال Present Tense :—

(*a*) فعل مطلق Present Indefinite.

(*b*) فعل ناتمام Present Imperfect.

(*c*) فعل تمام Present Perfect.

(*d*) فعل‌تمام جاري Present Perfect Continuous.

(*a*) فعل مطلق **Present Indefinite** refers strictly to a present time and to single acts or habits without regard to duration, as میں آتا ہوں I come, میں پیار کرتا ہوں I love.

(*b*) فعل نا تمام **Present Imperfect** denotes an action going on and not finished. It is formed by adding رہا to the Root followed by ہوں - ہے - ہیں یا ہو, as میں پیار کررہا ہوں I am loving, etc.

(*c*) فعل تمام **Present Perfect** indicates an action that has just now finished. In Intransitive Verb

ھوں - ھے - ھیں or ھو is added to the Past Tense, as میں گیا ھوں I have gone. وہ گیا ھے He has gone. In Transitive Verb ھے and ھیں is added to the Past Tense, as میں نے گھوڑے دیکھے ھیں I have seen horses. میں نے روٹی کھائی ھے I have eaten bread.

(*d*) فعل تمام جاری **Present Perfect Continuous** expresses an action begun at some past time and continued up to the time specified in the tense, as میں کرتا رھا ھوں I have been doing. تو پیار کرتا رھا ھے Thou hast been loving.

(3) فعل مضارع The Aorist.

فعل مضارع **The Aorist** denotes an action which indicates Present and Future Tenses, as جائے - آئے کھائے etc. After dropping 'نا' the sign of مصدر Root add یائے مجہول if after dropping the sign of مصدر there is 'الف' or 'واو' or 'یائے مجہول' add 'ھمزہ' and یائے مجہول as آئے from انا - کھائے from کھانا , دوڑے from دوڑنا etc.

صیغے The Gender, Number and Person of فعل مضارع Aorist are the same for Masculine and Feminine both.

واحد حاضر	جمع متکلم	واحد متکلم	
تو آئے	ہم آئیں	میں آؤں	مذکر و مونث
جمع غائب	واحد غائب	جمع حاضر	
وے آئیں	وہ آئے	تم آؤ	مذکر و مونث

(4) فعل مستقبل Future Tense

فعل مستقبل **Future Tense** is formed by adding گا to the فعل مضارع Aorist.

Masculine and Feminine.

	Singular.	*Plural.*
1st Per.	میں آؤنگا - آؤنگی	ہم آئینگے - آئینگی
	I shall come	We shall come
2nd Per.	تو آئیگا - آئیگی	تم آؤگے - آؤگي
	Thou wilt come	You will come
3rd Per.	وہ آئیگا - آئیگي	وے آئینگے - آئینگی
	He / She } will come	They will come

(5) فعل امر The Imperative.

(1) **The Imperative** indicates command or instructions. It is used only in واحد حاضر, *2nd* Person.

(2) The Singular form of Imperative is itself the root of the Verb, as سو - کھا - جا - آ etc. as تو جا Go thou. تو کر Do thou.

(3) او is added to the root in the Plural form as تم کھاؤ You eat. تم جاؤ You go.

(4) Sometimes فعل امر Imperative indicates continuance. Such امر is called مدامي as آتا رہ امر مدامی—کھاتا رہ is formed by adding تا رہ in the امر Imperative, as آتا رہ - بھاگتا رہ -

(5) For respect instead of او - یئے is added to the roots, as آپ آیئے Please (you) come. جایئے - کھایئے etc. Sometimes گا is added to this, as آیئے گا - چلیئیگا etc. Sometimes for emphasis مصدر is used as کھنا یاد رکھنا - جانا ہاں etc.

(6) فعل نہي The Negative Imperative.

فعل نہی The Negative Imperative is that which forbids somebody to do something, as مت آ - مت آو - نہ جاؤ - نہ جا - نہ کھاؤ - نہ کھا - نہ -

Sometimes مت or نہ is used before مصدر and then it gives the sense ot Future tense, as نہ ڈرنا - مت جانا

4. متعدي فعلوں كي گردان

Conjugation of Transitive Verbs.

Transitive Verbs have two forms :—

معروف **Active Voice** and مجہول **Passive Voice**

(1) صورت معروف **Active Voice** denotes that the فاعل Subject of the Verb acts, as رام نے سانپ کو مارا Ram killed a snake.

(2) صورت مجہول **Passive Voice** denotes that the فاعل Subject of the Verb is acted upon, as سانپ رام سے مارا گیا A snake was killed by Rama.

(*a*) The مفعول Object in the صورت معروف Active Voice becomes the فاعل Subject in the صورت مجہول Passive Voice.

(*b*) In the Conjugation of فعل لازم Intransitive Verb excepting مضارع Aorist, امر Imperative and نهي Negative Imperative there are different صیغے Persons, for the Genders of all the Verbs and changes take place in the فعل Verb, as - وہ آتا - وہ آتی - وے آتے وے آتیں etc.

(*c*) In the فعل ماضي نا تمام Past Imperfect فعل ماضي تمناي Conditional Past, فعل حال Present, فعل

مضارع Aorist and فعل مستقبل Future as regards Gender, Number and Person of the Subject, changes take place just as in the Conjugation of the فعل لازم Intransitive Verb, whether there be one, two or three objects of the Transitive Verb.

(*d*) In the حالتوں Cases of Nouns it has been mentioned that in the ماضی مطلق Past Indefinite, ماضی قریب Present Perfect, ماضي بعيد Past and ماضي شكيه Doubtful Past Tense of فعل متعدي Transitive Verb when a Noun is the فاعل Subject the sign of Nominative 'نے' comes with it, and so if the Nominative is a Pronoun sign نے shall come with it also, as هم نے سبق پڑھا We read the lesson.

(*e*) If there is 'نے' in a sentence and there is not 'کو' the sign of Objective the changes in the فعل Verb shall be according to مفعول Objective, as - رام نے کتاب پڑھی - میں نے روٹي کھائي - اسنے کھانا کھایا -

(*f*) When the فعل متعدي Transitive Verb has two Objects the فعل Verb shall be according to the 2nd Object, as هم نے لڑکي کو ایك پیسا دیا - دو پیسے دیئے - روٹی دي - روٹیاں دیں

(*g*) When the فعل متعدی has three مفعول Objects the فعل Verb shall be according to the 3rd Object, as روتي دلوائی - دو پیسے دلوائے - ہم نے لڑکی کو پیسہ دلوایا - روتیاں دلوائیں

(*h*) When the sign of مفعول Objective is in the sentence the ماضی مطلق - ماضی قریب - بعید - شکیہ will always be واحد مذکر Singular Masculine, as باپ نے بلي نے چوھے کو کھایا- استاد نے لڑکے کو مارا- لڑکوں کو مارا بلیوں نے چوھے کو کھایا - etc. etc.

(*i*) To form the مصدر مجہول from the مصدر معروف add the word 'جانا' after صیغہ واحد مذکر of ماضي مطلق Past Indefinite, as مارا جانا from مارنا - کیا جانا from کرنا etc.

(*j*) To form the فعل مجہول Passive from the مصدر معروف add that فعل Verb which is to be made from مصدر معروف after its ماضی مطلق , if ماضي قریب مجہول Present Perfect Passive is to be formed take the ماضي مطلق of مارنا first which is مارا , after it add ماضی قریب Present Perfect of مصدر جانا thus 'مارا کیا ھے' is formed. This is the ماضی قریب مجہول Present Perfect Passive.

فعل کی چند خاص صورتیں
5.—Some Particular Forms of Verbs.

A

نفی فعل Negative Verbs.

The **Negative** form is used for *denying.* It requires نہ or نہیں not, as وہ نہ گیا He did not go ; وہ نہیں جاتا ہے He does not go, تم نہیں جاؤ گے You will not go.

B

مرکب فعل Compound Verbs

فعل مستقبل تمام Future Perfect is formed by adding ' چکے گا ' before امر Imperative, as کھا چکیگا from کھانا . آچکیگا from آنا .

فعل حال نا تمام Present Imperfect and فعل مستقبل نا تمام Future Imperfect are thus formed :—Put after امر Imperative and ماضی تمنائی Conditional Past the Present and Future of 'رہنا,' as آ رہا ہے Present Imperfect from آنا and Future Imperfect " آتا رہیگا "

C

فعل تاکیدی Emphatic Form of Verb.

When from any مصدر Root تاکیدی صورت **Emphatic Form** of the Verb is to be made, use the same Verb of مصدر Root جانا - لینا - ڈالنا - دینا etc. after the Imperative 2nd Person Singular of that مصدر as وہ آیا He came—(emphatic) وہ گیا He did come. سنا heard—(emphatic) سن لیا did hear ; کہا said—(emphatic) کہہ دیا did say, etc.

D

اختیاري صورت Potential Form.

In Urdu سکنا 'can' is the word which expresses power. اختیاري صورت The **Potential Form** is formed by adding the Verb of سکنا مصدر of which this form is to be made after the Imperative 2nd Person Singular, as میں یہہ کر سکتا ہوں I can do it, اب وہ جا سکتا ھے He can go now.

E

فعل معاون Auxiliary Verbs.

The Verbs which are used in forming Compound Verbs are called فعل معاون Auxiliary Verbs, as جانا - دینا - لینا - ڈالنا - چکنا - سکنا - رهنا etc.

F

فعل معطوف Compound Perfect Participle.

In Urdu sometimes two فعل Verbs come together and between them 'کر' or 'کے' The first word is called معطوف علیہ and the second معطوف as وہ روٹي

کھا کر گیا Eating his bread he went ; 'کھا ' is معطوف and 'گیا ' معطوف علیہ مجھے گرا کر وہ بھاگ گیا — Throwing me down he ran away. 'گرا ' معطوف and 'بھاگ گیا ' معطوف علیہ

فعل معطوف Compound Perfect Participle is formed by using ' کر ' or ' کے ' after a 2nd Person Singular Imperative Verb and adding another Verb after them.

G

مصدر Infinitive.

It has already been explained above that مصدر کھانا - ھونا - کرنا etc. have no tense. In Urdu, like Persian, it is supposed to be Noun and can be in the Nominative, Objective and Possessive Cases. With the متعدی مصدر Transitive Infinitive there should be its objective also, as اُس کا لڑکے کو مارنا اچھا نہیں ھے His beating the child is not good. Here ' لڑکا ' child is the object of مصدر ' مارنا '.

H

شبہہ فعل Participles.

Some forms of Verbs partaking the properties of the Verb and the Adjective are called شبہہ فعل **Participles**.

They are three :—

(1) صفت فاعل **Participle or Noun of Agency.**

(2) صفت مفعول **Perfect Participle.**

(3) صفت حالیہ **Imperfect Participle.**

(1) صفت فاعل **Participle or Noun of Agency.**

صفت فاعل **Participle of Agency** is the quality of the doer of an action obtained from its relation to that action, as پڑھنے والا - کھانے والا - جانے والا etc.

For forming the صفت فاعل Participle of Agency change the ' الف ' of مصدر into یائے مجہول and add والا, as کھانے والا from کھانا, سونے والا from سونا, مرنے والا from مرنا.

Some Persian Participles of Agency have been used in Urdu in which very little sense of quality is found, as چرندہ (چرنے والا), پرندہ (اُڑنے والا), etc.

Some Compound **Participles** of Agency are used as صفت Adjectives, as گنہگار sinner, دولتمند rich, ہنرمند skilful, غمگین sad, خشم ناك wrathful, etc. Arabic Participle of Agency is also used in Urdu, as عالم learned, ظالم tyrant, منصف just, etc.

(2) صفت مفعول Perfect Participle.

صفت مفعول **Perfect Participle** is the quality of the person acted upon. It is formed of فعل متعدی Transitive Verb by adding ہوا to the Past Indefinite Tense, as لکھا ہوا written, مارا ہوا struck.

Sometimes ہوا is added to the فعل لازم Intransitive Verb in the ماضی مطلق Past Indefinite Tense. The action having finished it becomes the quality of the doer, as گرا ہوا fallen, ڈوبا ہوا drowned, سویا ہوا slept, کھویا ہوا lost. It is called صفت ماضیہ **Past Participle**.

Some Perfect Participles are used in Urdu, as آمیختہ mixed, compound, سوختہ burnt, مردہ dead, etc.

Some Arabic صفت مفعول are used in Urdu, as مصروف busy, معلوم known, مظلوم oppressed, موقوف stopped, etc.

(3) صفت حالیہ Imperfect Participle.

صفت حالیہ **Imperfect Participle** is that which indicates the condition of Nominative or Objective. It is formed by adding تا or تے after deleting نا the sign of مصدر Infinitive, as سوتا sleeping from سونا sleep,

روتا weeping from رونا, weep, etc. Sometimes هوا or هوئے is also added to تا or تے, as جلتا هوا walking, كهاتا هوا or كهاتے هوئے eating, هنستے هوئے laughing from هنسنا laugh میں نے اسے سوتا یا سوتا هوا یا سوتے هوئے پایا I found him sleeping, میں نے لچھمن کو هنستے هوئے دیکھا I saw Lachhman laughing.

مرکب فعل کي مثالیں

Examples of Compound Verbs or Dual.

Two فعل مرکب combined Verbs are used to intensify the meaning of the expression. In all such combined words the first Verb is the root and is not changed, only the 2nd Verb can be inflected. Such words, as پڑنا - لینا - دینا - ڈالنا, etc. are generally used as the second Verb.

لینا—*To take.*

لوٹ لینا to rob	پہچان لینا to recognise
تھام لینا to hold up	سن لینا to listen
مان لینا to obey	چھین لینا to snatch
جان لینا to come to know	سنبھال لینا to manage
کاٹ لینا to bite	اُٹھا لینا to take up

etc., etc.

دینا—*To give.*

کھو دینا to lose
کہہ دینا to say
دے دینا to give
بھیج دینا to send away
چھوڑ دینا to leave
جلا دینا to burn
ڈال دینا to throw away
لوٹا دینا to give back
مار دینا to strike
نکال دینا to turn out

etc., etc.

پڑنا—*To fall.*

It expresses 'suddenness', as :

گر پڑنا to fall down
رو پڑنا to weep out
ٹوٹ پڑنا to rush upon
اُچھل پڑنا to jump up
نکل پڑنا to go out
چونك پڑنا to be startled
دوڑ پڑنا to run down
ھنس پڑنا to laugh out

etc., etc.

جانا—*To go.*

It is used as a second Verb to denote 'completion of an action,' as :

کھا جانا to eat up
نگل جانا to swallow down
بھول جانا to forget
جان جانا to get to know
مر جانا to die away
سو جانا to sleep down
لے جانا to carry away
ھو جانا to become
چلا جانا to go away
گر جانا to fall down

etc., etc.

أٹھنا—*To get up.*

It expresses the 'sense of sudden action', as :

چونك أٹھنا to start up	جاگ اٹھنا to wake up
چلا اٹھنا to cry out	بول أٹھنا to speak out

etc., etc.

بیٹھنا—*To sit.*

It expresses 'haste in action', as :

کر بیٹھنا to do	مار بیٹھنا to beat
پوچھه بیٹھنا to interrogate	کھو بیٹھنا to lose

etc., etc.

رکھنا—چھوڑنا—*To keep, to abandon*

بیٹھا رکھنا to detain	رکھه چھوڑنا to keep
روك رکھنا to stop	چھوڑ رکھنا to leave out
کہہ رکھنا to keep informed	چھپا رکھنا to keep concealed or hidden
تیار رکھنا to keep ready	

etc., etc.

ڈالنا—*To throw.*

کھا ڈالنا to devour up	کات ڈلنا to cut up
توڑ ڈالنا to break up	پہن ڈالنا to wear over

مار ڈالنا to kill away مٹا ڈالنا to efface
دے ڈالنا to give up اُڑا ڈالنا to squander

etc., etc.

فعل معاون کے استعمال

Uses of Auxiliary Verbs

In Conjugation the principal Verb remains unchanged but the **Auxiliary Verb** is subject to Inflection.

(*i*) چکنا—is added to the root to express 'finish or completion', as :

وہ کھا چکا, He finished eating
میں پڑھ چکا I finished reading.
میں سوچکا I finished sleeping.
میں کہہ چکا ہوں I have finished.
ہم بول چکے تھے We had spoken.
وہ بھیج چکے ہونگے They might have sent

etc., etc.

(*ii*) پانا—is used after the root of a Verb or with modified infinitive to express 'to be able to', as :

کرنے پانا - کرپانا to be able to do

پہونچنے پایا or میں وهاں نهیں پهونچ پایا
I could not reach there.

دیکھنے پاؤگے or تم نهیں دیکهه پاؤگے You will not be able to see.

etc., etc.

(*iii*) چاهنا—is used to express 'want or desire,' as :

میں کهیلنا چاهتا هوں I want to play.

تم کیا بولنا چاهتے هو What do you want to speak.

etc., etc.

(*iv*) دینا—is used with the مصدر Infinitive but the last سنا of مصدر is changed into ے, as :

اسنے مجھے جانے دیا He permitted me to go.

مجھے کهنے دیجئے Let me say.

مجھے سونے دو Let me sleep.

etc., etc.

(*v*) سکنا—is added to the root of the مصدر, as :

میں جاسکتا هوں I can go.

میں کیا کر سکتا هوں What can I do ?

وے نهیں آسکینگے They will not be able to come.

(vi) لیا—is used to express 'completion of an action', as :

میں نے کھانا کھالیا I have taken my dinner.

اسنے خط پڑہ لیا He has read the letter.

میں نے کپڑا خریدلیا I have purchased the cloth.

اسنے بي - اے پاس کرکیا She has passed the B. A.

etc., etc.

(vii) لگا—is used with the modified مصدر Infinitive, as :

وہ پڑھنے لگا He began to read.

سوھن رونے لگا Sohan began to weep.

وے بھاگنے لگے They began to run.

etc., etc.

Uses of some important Idiomatic Words and Particles.

چاھنا—It is used with Past Tense and expresses 'danger and immediate desire', as :

وہ مرا چاھتاھے He is at the point of death.

وہ بھاگا چاھتا ھے He is about to run away.

گھر گرا چاهتا هے The house is about to fall

etc., etc.

رهنا—It expresses that some action is continued. It is used with Participle, as :

وه کهیلتا رهتاهے He continues to play.

وه سوتا رهتا هے He continues to sleep.

تم بڑبڑاتے رهتے هو You go on murmuring.

etc., etc.

جانا—is used with modified Participle and expresses going on of an action, as -

وه هنستا جاتا هے He goes on laughing.

میں پڑهتا جاتا هوں I go on reading.

میں بولتا جاتا هوں I go on speaking.

تم لکهتے جاؤ You go on writing.

گا—is added to the فعل امر Imperative Verbs showing respect and it denotes an action to be done in future, as :

آپ کل ضرور آئیگا You will please come to-morrow without fail.

وهاں پهونچنے پر آپ خط بهیجئیگا You will please send me a letter on reaching there.

آئیو - جائیو وغیرہ—are also used as امر مستقبل Future Imperative. Such words show Familiarity, as:

تم میرے ساتھ چلیو You will go with me.

تم شام کو آئیو You will come in the evening.

هي—is a very important particle and is used in different senses. It is used for emphasis and always follows the thing it emphasises. Ordinarily it means, 'only' or 'alone'.

(*i*) It expresses 'exclusiveness,' as:

میں هي I alone	دو هی only two
وهي - وہ هی he alone	همیں-هم هی we alone
یہیں-یہاں هی here only	سبھی-سب هي all
تبهي-تب هی then only	توهی thou alone
وے هی they alone	etc.

(*ii*) It expresses just the moment an act is performed, as:

میرے آتے هی وہ چلا گیا As soon as I came he went away.

نہاتے هی میرے سر میں درد هونے لگا As soon as I had a bath I felt headache.

ریل سے اترتے هی وہ مر گئی As soon as she got down the train she died.

(*iii*) With a Relative Pronoun it indicates 'the same', as :

یہی لڑکا ہے جو میرے گھر اتوار کو آیا تھا This is the boy who came at my place on Sunday.

پڑنا—It expresses 'force and compulsion', as :

مجھے روپئے ادھار لینا پڑے I had to borrow money.

مجھے دوائی کھانی پڑی I had to take medicine.

اسے بمبئی جانا پڑا He had to go to Bombay.

ہوگا- ہے - تھا تمہیں کرنا ہوگا- You will have to do.

مجھے جانا ہوگا I will have to go.

رام کو آج جانا تھا Rama had to go to-day.

مجھے واپس آنا ہے I have to come back.

etc., etc.

لگنا—It is used in different senses :

(*i*) It means 'to be in contact with,' as :

ھاتھ لگنا to come in hand

گلے لگنا to embrace

دل لگنا (midd) to attach to fall, in love

برا لگنا to take ill.

(*ii*) Hurtful contact, as :

گولی لگنا to be shot by a bullet

ٹھوکر لگنا to come violently in contact with something.

دھکا لگنا to have a shock

(*iii*) It expresses ' nearness and taste ,' as :

میرا گھر اسکے گھر سے لگا ھوا ھے My house is close to his house.

کھٹا لگنا to taste sour

کڑوا لگنا to taste bitter

اچھا لگنا to feel pleasant

تن بدن میں آگ لگنا to be indignant.

(*iv*) It means ' to begin ', as :

مارنے لگنا to begin beating

رونے لگنا to begin weeping

کھانے لگنا to begin eating

(*v*) It shows ' relation , as :

وہ میرا بھتیجہ لگتا ھے He is my nephew in relationship.

(*vi*) Many other uses of لگنا and لگانا

لگانا—it is Transitive of لگنا, as :

دل لگانا to pay attention | تیل لگانا to apply oil
یاری لگانا to make friendship | چھاتا لگانا to open an umbrella
چکر لگانا to go round | پیڑ لگانا to plant a tree
الزام لگانا to blame | بھوک لگنا to feel hungry
ٹکٹکی لگانا to gaze at | پیاس لگنا to feel thirsty
دام لگانا to bid the price of | تالا لگانا to lock up
پتا لگانا to trace out, to find out | حساب لگانا to calculate

بھر—It expresses the 'fullness and completeness,' as :

رات بھر the whole night | خاندان بھر the whole family
مٹھی بھر a handful | تولہ بھر as much as a tola
طاقت بھر with all power | پیٹ بھر stomachful, bellyful
زندگی بھر throughout life | جی بھر کے to one's heart's content

چاھئے—It expresses 'want', as :

تمکو کیا چاھئے What do you want ?

مجھے چھٹی چاھئے I want leave.

ھیرا کو ایک روپیہ چاھئے Hira wants a rupee.

بلا—It means 'without,' as :

بلا غسل کئے without bathing

بلا کھاے without eating

بلا اجازت without permission

بلا خوف without fear.

سا—It expresses 'likeness' and is Subject to number and gender of nouns, as :

وہ محمد بخش سا نظر آتا هے He looks like Mohammad Bakhsh.

میں نے تمھارا سا آدمی نهیں دیکھا I have not seen a man like you.

ایك گوری سی عورت A fair-looking woman.

اسکي آواز لڑکي کی سی هے His voice is like that of a girl.

[*Note*—سا is also used after چھوٹا - بڑا - بہت-کون - تھوڑا but it does not alter the meaning and has no special significance.]

نه—Besides using نه in Negative

(i) it is used in the Interrogative sense like the English 'Isn't it', as :

یہہ گھر تمہارا ھے نہ This house is yours, isn't it?

کل رات تمھي ميرا گھر کھٹکھٹا رھے تھے نہ You were knocking my door last night, isn't it?

کل تم ڈاك سے جاؤ گے نہ You will go by mail to-morrow, isn't it?

(*ii*) It is also used for 'neither or nor', as:

میرے پاس نہ موٹر ھے نہ ٹانگا I have neither a motor nor a tonga.

نہ تم آے نہ وہ آیا Neither he came nor you.

ھوتا ھے—It is used to express a 'natural truth and custom', as:

ھبشی کالے ھوتے ھیں Negroes are black.

پرندوں کے دو بازو ھوتے ھیں Birds have two wings.

رات کو تاریکي ھوتي ھے It is dark in the night.

اس گھر میں روز ناچنے گانے کا جشن ھوتا ھے Dancing and singing takes place daily in this house.

تو—It is very commonly used for emphasis. In English there are different words for expressing the sense equivalent to تو , as :

میں بھي تو آتا هوں I too am going of course.

وہ جانتا تو ہے He does know.

میں پڑھتا تو ہوں I do read.

هاں تو Yes of course.

نہیں تو Of course not.

معاملہ تو یہي ہے The matter of course is this.

میں تو تھا آگے اور تم تھے پیچھے I was of course (in front) and you were behind.

آپ نے مجھے حکم دیا تھا نہیں تو میں وهاں کیوں جاتا You ordered me or else why should have I gone there.

نہ تو تم خود کرتے ہو نہ کرنے دیتے ہو. You neither do yourself nor allow me to do.

تم جانتے تو ہو. You certainly know, don't you ?

آج دفتر بند تو نہیں ہے To-day the office is not closed, isn't it ?

تم جاتے تو نہیں ہو. You are not going, are you ?

میں جانتا تو ہوں پر بتاؤ لگا نہیں I do know but I won't tell.

وہ مجھسے کہتے تو صحیح کہ وہ کیا چاہتا ہے

He may tell me truly what he wants.

تم اسکو ایک بار لکھو بھی تو صحیح Just write him once.

ذرا بتاو تو صحیح وہ کہاں رہتے ہیں Just say where he lives.

etc., etc.

STUDY OF WORDS

Inflection of Some Verbs

LESSON 1.

فعل حال *Present*	فعل ماضی *Past*	صفت ماضیہ *Past Participle*
پڑھنا read	پڑھا read	پڑھا ہوا read
بند کرنا shut	بند کیا shut	بند کیا ہوا shut
کاٹنا cut	کاٹا cut	کاٹا ہوا cut
پھیلانا - بچھانا spread	پھیلایا - بچھایا spread	پھیلایا-بچھایا ہوا spread
جاگنا awake	جاگا awoke	جاگا ہوا awaked
ہونا be	تھا was	ہوا been

Present	*Past*	*Past Participle*
مارنا beat	مارا beat	مارا هوا beaten
شروع کرنا begin	شروع کیا began	شروع کیا هوا begun
کاٹنا (دانت سے) bite	کاٹا bit	کاٹا هوا bitten
توڑنا break	توڑا broke	توڑا هوا broken
آنا come	آیا came	آیا هوا come
پینا drink	پیا drank	پیا هوا drunk
کھانا eat	کھایا ate	کھایا هوا eaten
معاف کرنا forgive	معاف کیا forgave	معاف کیا هوا forgiven
دینا give	دیا gave	دیا هوا given
جانا go	گیا went	گیا هوا gone
دوڑنا run	دوڑا ran	دوڑا هوا run
دیکھنا see	دیکھا saw	دیکھا هوا seen
دکھلانا show	دکھلایا showed	دکھلایا هوا shown
بولنا speak	بولا spoke	بولا هوا spoken
خرچ کرنا spend	خرچ کیا spent	خرچ کیا هوا spent
پھٹنا burst	پھٹا burst	پھٹا هوا burst
قرض دینا lend	قرض دیا lent	قرض دیا هوا lent

LESSON 2.

Present	*Past*	*Past Participle*
گانا sing	گایا sang	گایا هوا sung
تیرنا swam	تیرا swam	تیرا هوا swum
اُڑنا fly	اُڑا flown	اُڑا هوا flown
جانا know	جانا knew	جانا هوا known
اُگنا grow	اُگا grew	اُگا هوا grown
لکهنا write	لکها wrote	لکها هوا written
لانا - پانا	لایا - پایا	پایا هوا - لایا هوا
get	got	gotten
تهوکنا spit	تهوکا spat	تهوکا هوا spit
لینا take	لیا took	لیا هوا taken
چرانا steal	چرایا stole	چرایا هوا stolen
کرنا do	کیا did	کیا هوا done
بیچنا sell	بیچا sold	بیچا هوا sold
کہنا say	کہا said	کہا هوا said
بنانا make	بنایا made	بنا هوا made
بیٹهنا sit	بیٹها sat	بیٹها هوا sat
کهڑا هونا stand	کهڑا هوا stood	کهڑا هوا stood
گرنا fall	گرا fell	گرا هوا fallen

LESSON 3.

Present	*Past*	*Past Participle*
اُٹھنا rise	اُٹھا rose	اُٹھا هوا risen
سکڑنا shrink	سکڑا shrank	سکڑا هوا shrunk
قسم کهانا swear	قسم کهائی swore	قسم کهایا هوا sworn.
بننا weave	بنا wove	بنا هوا woven
مارنا strike	مارا struck	مارا هوا struck, stricken
بهاگنا flee	بهاگا fled	بهاگا هوا fled
سینا sew	سیا sewed	سیا هوا sewn
رکهنا have	رکها had	رکها هوا had
پهونکنا blow	پهونکا blew	پهونکا هوا blown
پهاڑنا tear	پهاڑا tore	پهاڑا هوا torn
منت کرنا beseech	منت کي besought	منت کیا هوا besought
ملنا meet	ملا met	ملا هوا met
ڈوبنا - دهسنا sink	ڈوبا - دهسا sank	ڈوبا هوا - دهسا هوا sunk
سکهانا teach	سکهایا taught	سکهایا هوا taught
پهیلانا spill	پهیلا spilt	پهیلا هوا spilt
سوچنا think	سوچا thought	سوچا هوا thought

CHAPTER VIII.

V.—صلہ فعل The ADVERB.

Words used mostly with a verb explaining its meaning are called صلہ فعل **Adverb.** صلہ فعل Adverbs may be divided into different classes according to their meaning :—

(1 زمان فعل **Adverbs of Time.** They express the time of action, as اب now, تب then, جب when, تک till, پہلے before, ہمیشہ always, کبھی کبھی sometimes. اگر اب نہ آیا تو کب آونگا If he did not come *now*, when *will* he come.

(2) مکان فعل **Adverbs of Place.** They express the place of an action, as یہاں here, وہاں there, ادھر hither, کدھر whither, نزدیک near, آگے before, etc. لچھمن یہاں بیٹھا ہے Lachhman is sitting *here*, etc.

(3) مقدر فعل **Adverbs of Quantity.** They denote the quantity of a Verb, as اتنا زیادہ so much, more, قریب قریب almost, قریباً nearly, خاصکر chiefly, particularly, بالکل quite, etc. آج زیادہ مینھہ برسا It rained *much* to-day, وہ بالکل اچھا ہے He is *quite* well, اتنا نہ لو Don't take *so much*.

(4) نتیجہ فعل , سبب **Adverbs of Cause and Effect.** They express why an act was done, as کیوں why, بےشک certainly, واقعی indeed, etc. تم وھاں کیوں گئے *Why* did you go there? بے شک میں وھاں جاؤنگا *Certainly* I will go there.

(5) وضع فعل **Adverbs of Manner.** They express the manner of an action, as ایسے thus, جیسے as, یکایک suddenly, جھٹ immediately, جلد quickly, etc. ایسے یا یوں کرو Do it *thus.* جھٹ سے آؤ Come *immediattey*, etc.

(6) انکار , جواب **Adverbs of Affirmation and Negation.** They express affirmation and negation, as اچھا all right, ھاں yes, نہیں no, کیا what, etc نہیں میں نہ جاؤنگا *No* I will *not* go, ھاں تم اُسے لے سکتے ھو *Yes,* you can have it. اچھا میں چلا جاؤنگا *All right*, I will go away.

(7) صفت تفصیل **Adverbs of Quality.** They express quality of Verb and Adjective, as بہت یہ بہت اچھا سیب ھے This is a *very* good apple, رام بہت ھی ھوشیار لڑکا ھے Ram is a *very* clever boy. وہ جلدی لکھتا ھے He writes *fast.*

STUDY OF WORDS.

LESSON 1.

کبھی ever	کبھی نہیں never
نیچے below	باھر outside
جتنا as much	کتنا how much
مت don't	بلا شك undoubtedly
اس باعث on this account	کب when
جبکہ awhile	جلد soon
گذرے ago	فورا instantly
پہلے سے already	اوپر above
آج to-day	کل to-morrow
روز مرہ daily	شاد و نادر seldom
ھر جگھہ everywhere	اندر inside

بے وقوفی سے foolishly

LESSON 2.

بہت very	نہایت too
اسمیں therein	اُسپر thereat
جبکہ whereas	اس سے thereby
اب سے آگے henceforth	جہاں کہیں wherever

اسپر hereupon	اسکا hereof
اس سے hereby	آگے کو hereafter
اسی طرح likewise	کسی طرح نہیں by no means
کم سے کم at least	علاوہ بریں besides
بے فائدہ in vain	آخر کار at last
عموماً in general	خصوصاً in particular
ادھر اودھر to and fro	مختصراً in short
حالمیں lately	اور کہیں elsewhere
منجملہ altogether	نہایت exceedingly
بلکہ rather	ایک بار once
دوبار twice	بموجب accordingly
تاهم still	شاید perhaps

بہ نسبت than

VI.—حرف جار The PREPOSITION.

Words which show the relation in which the person or thing denoted by it stands to something else. In Urdu such words are placed after a Noun or Pronoun, as وہ گھر میں ھے He is *in* the house. کتاب میز پر ھے The book is *on* the table.

Following are the حرف جار **Prepositions.** They are known as case-terminations, as کو to, میں in,

سے from, کے لئے for کا - کی - کے of, as آپکو to you, مجھکو to me, گھر میں in the house, سوھن سے from Sohan, احمد کے لئے for Ahmad.

In Possessive case-termination کا is used when the اسم Noun following is مذکر Masculine, as بابو کا گھوڑا Babu's horse, in Plural کا shall be changed into کے and گھوڑا into گھوڑے, as بابوکےگھوڑے Babu's horses, For مونث Feminine it is changed into یاے مجہول, as سوھن کی لڑکی The daughter of Sohan.

Post-position.

The following words are called Post-positions because they are preceded by 'کے' or 'کی'

نیچے below	بھیتر inside
پاس near	ساتھ with
بغیر without	پہلے before
سامنے in front	بعد after
بابت about	طرف towards
مانند like	سواے except

اوپر above

as میز کے نیچے below the table, گھر کے باھر out of house چھت کے اوپر above the roof, میرے گھر کے پاس near my house.

مانند like, طرف towards are preceded by 'کی' as پورب کی طرف towards east, کتے کی طرح like a dog.

Some idiomatic uses of Case terminations.

'سے' comes before the following فعل Verbs :—

(کسي) سے وعدہ کرنا to promise, (کسي) سے شادي کرنا to marry, (کسی) سے کہنا to tell, (کسی) سے مانگنا to beg, (کسی) سے ملاقات کرنا to meet, (کسی) سے انکار کرنا to refuse. Sometimes 'سے' is omitted, as کانوں سننا to hear, آنکھوں دیکھنا to see, بھوکوں مرنا to starve, etc.

اضافت Possessives کا - کے - کی are used :

(*i*) To show the value of a thing, as دس روپئے کی کتاب A book costing ten rupees, دس ھزار روپئے کا مکان A house costing ten thousand rupees, چار آنہ کے امرود Four annas worth guavas.

(*ii*) To show age, as اسی برس کا Eighty years of age, ایک برس کے بچے One year old infants, چار برس کی لڑکی A girl of four years.

Some فعل Verbs take 'پر' before them, as :

مجھہ پر مہربانی کرو Be kind to me.

اُس پر بھروسہ رکھو Trust him.

مجھے اُس پر شک ہے I doubt him.

اُس پر ناراض نہ ہو Don't be angry with him.

شیر نے مجھہ پر حملہ کیا The lion attacked me.

Double Case-terminations are often used to express 'میں سے out of' and 'پر سے from' respectively, as :

پچاس امیدواروں میں سے. Out of fifty candidates.

میري جیب میں سے Out of my pocket.

اسکے صندق میں سے From his box.

مکان کے چھت پر سے From the roof of the house.

پیڑ پر سے From the tree.

STUDY OF WORDS

ساتھہ with	بعد after
سامنے in front	بارے میں - بابت about, regarding
مانند-طرح - موافق like	
بیچ میں among	پرے beyond
وار پار across	اوپر over
نیچے beneath, down	خلاف against
ساتھہ ساتھہ along	سواء except

قبل before　　　　سے from

واسطے for　　　　کو to

کا of　　　　میں in

طرف - جانب towards.

VII.—حرف عطف The CONJUNCTION.

Words which join two words and sentences are called حرف عطف Conjunctions, as تم جا سکتے ہو مگر مجھے ٹھہرنا ضرور ہے You can go *but* I must stay. دو اور دو چار ہوتے ہیں Two *and* two make four. In these examples 'مگر' *but* joins the sentences, as 'تم جاسکتے ہو You can go' and 'مجھے ٹھہرنا ضرور ہے I must stay'. The word 'اور *and*' joins the words, دو اور دو Two and two. حرف عطف Conjunction joins the words of the same Parts of Speech—Noun with Noun, Adverb with Adverb, etc.

The first Word or Sentence is called معطوف الیہ and the other معطوف.

حرف عطف **Conjunctions** are of two kinds :—

حرف اتصال **Copulative** is that which joins sentences and meanings.

حرف انفصال **Disjunctive** is that which joining the sentences separates the meaning.

1.—حرف اِتصال **Copulative Conjunctions** are of three kinds :—

(1) جمع **Cumulative Conjunction** joins two words and sentences in one condition, as پتھر اور متی جان آیا اور بے جان ھیں Stone and earth are lifeless. جیمس چلا گیا John came and James went away. They are :

اور and　　بھی also　　اور - بھی as well as

پھر again　　پس so　　نہ صرف not only, etc.

(2) حرف شرط **Conjunctions of Condition, Supposition or Qualification** join such sentences which are dependent on each other. They are :

اگر if　　اگرچہ though

وگر نہ if not　　جب تک کہ نہ unless

گویا کہ as if　　سواے except

بلا without　　بشرطیکہ provided that

خواہ whether　　باوجودیکہ notwithstanding

فرض کرو کہ supposing that, etc.

as : وہ ایماندار آدمی ھے اگرچہ غریب ھے He is an honest man *though* he is poor, میں اُسکا احسانمند ھونگا اگر

وہ اپنی کتاب دے دیوے, I shall be obliged to him *if* he will lend me the book.

(3) حرف بیان **Conjuntions of End or Purpose** join two such sentences that the second may serve the end or purpose of the first, as رام نے کہا کہ آج میرا باپ بیمار ھے Ram said *that* to-day my father is ill.

2. حرف انفصال **Disjunctive** joins the sentences and separates the meaning. They are also of three kinds :

(1) حرف تردید **Exclusives** are those which coming between the words mean one of them. They are : یا or, خواہ whether, بلکہ rather, یا تو either, نہ تو neither, نہ nor.

(2) استدراك **Adversative Conjunctions** coming between the two sentences, the 2nd removes the doubt of the 1st.

They are : لیکن - پر but, الا - مگر however.

(3) حرف استثناء **Exceptional** is that conjunction which separates a Noun or Pronoun from the others, as موتی کے سوا سب لڑکے حاضر ھیں Except Moti all boys are present. They are سوا except, ما سوا besides.

STUDY OF WORDS

بھی also	اگرچہ - حالانکہ although	چونکہ - جیسا as
کیونکہ because	دونوں both	نہیں تو else
یاتو either	بھی even	مگر however
اگر if	شاید lest	نہ تو neither
نہ nor	باوجودیکہ notwithstanding	بشرطیکہ provided
بہ‌نسبت than	اس لئے therefore	جب تک unless
خواہ whether	تو بھی still	کہانسے whence
لہذا consequently	تاکہ so that	تب then

نہیں تو otherwise کہ that

VIII—حرف منشاء Interjection.

Words used to express some sudden feeling and emotion—joy, grief, surprise, indignation etc. are called حرف منشاء **Interjection.**

Uses of حرف منشاء Interjection.

(1) Some حرف منشاء are used for calling, as ابے او -ارےاو - او - ارے - اے : O brother اے بھائی اجی ھوت These are called حرف ندا

(2) Some express pain and sorrow, as وائے نصیب ھائے سخت درد ھے These are called حرف تاسف

(3) Some express wonder, as او - اوهو - ها These are called حرف تعجب

(4) Some express joy, as اهوهو - اهاها - اها واه واه, These are called حرف انبساط

(5) Some are used for praise, as صبحان و شاباش الله etc. These are called حرف تحسين

(6) Some are used for reproving and threatening, as هين - هشت - چهی - هوں

STUDY OF WORDS.

او - آه O, Oh	واه واه Huzza ; Hurrah
چپ Hush	شاباش - واه بهادر Bravo
اها Aha	هاها He ; ha
هلو Hullo	ديكهو Lo
چهی‌چهی - پو Pooh	الوداع Adieu
رخصتي سلام Farewell	مبارك هو Hail
شرم كي بات Shame	كيا What

etc.

PART III.

CHAPTER IX.

جملوں کي بناوت—Formation of Sentences.

Any number of words so joined as to have a complete meaning form a کلام or جمله Sentence, as روح کبهي نهيں مرتي The soul never dies. پرند اُڑتے هيں Birds fly. ميرا بهائي سوتا هے My brother is sleeping etc. etc.

1. With the Meaning point of view sentences are of two kinds :

(1) جمله خبريه Jumla Khabria.

(2) جمله انشائيه Jumla Inshaiya.

(1) جمله خبريه is that of which can be said it is true or false, as : رام ديال سبق پڑهتا هے Ram Dayal reads his lesson. ميں بيمار هوں I am sick, etc.

(2) جمله انشائيه is that of which true or false cannot be said, as ٹهنڈا پاني دو Give cold water. تم نه جاؤ You don't go.

2. Information of a sentence proper arrangement of words subject to Grammatical Rules is most essential.

3. There can be no جمله Sentence without a فعل Verb, therefore every sentence consists of two parts —مسند اليه Subject and مسند the **Predicate**.

مسند اليه The **Subject** is the person or thing spoken of, as آگ جلتي هے *Fire* burns, موهن اچها هے *Mohan* is well.

In these examples آگ *fire* and *Mohan* are مسند اليه Subjects.

مسند The **Predicate** is what is said about the مسند اليه Subject (person or thing) as, in the examples above 'اچها هے is well' and 'جلتي هے burns' are مسند Predicates.

4. With the Formation point of view sentences are of three kinds :—

A. جمله مفرد **Simple Sentence**.

B. جمله ملتف **Complex Sentence**.

C. جمله مركب **Compound Sentence**.

A. جمله مفرد **Simple Sentence**.

جمله مفرد A **Simple Sentence** contains only one مسند اليه **Subject** and one مسند **Predicate**, as پرند اڑتے هيں Birds fly. لڑكياں گاتي هيں Girls sing.

جملہ مفرد Simple Sentences are of two kinds :—

(*a*) جملہ اسمیہ **Jumla Ismiya.**

(*b*) جملہ فعلیہ **Jumla Feliya.**

(*a*)—جملہ اسمیہ **Jumla Ismiya.**

(1) جملہ اسمیہ is a sentence in which مسند الیہ Subject and مسند Predicate both are nouns. In جملہ اسمیہ-مسند الیہ Subject is called مبتدا and مسند Predicate خبر

(2) Sometimes ضمیر Pronoun شبہہ فعل Participle, and صفت Adjectives also are مبتدا Subjects and خبر Predicate is sometimes اسم Noun, صفت Adjective, ضمیر Pronoun and شبہہ فعل Participle.

(3) In the جملہ اسمیہ there is a فعل Verb besides مبتدا and خبر which joins both of them. It is called کلمۂ ربط Copula, as ھے - ھیں - ھو - ھوں etc.

(4) When مبتدا Subject is واحد, Singular the کلمۂ ربط Copula 'ھے is' is used, and in جمع plural 'ھیں are' but in Singular 1st Person 'ھوں' and 2nd Person Plural 'ھو' are used.

(5) When مبتدا Subject and خبر Predicate say something done in the Past Tense کلمۂ ربط copulas 'ھے is, ھیں are' are changed into 'تھا was, تھے were' according to the gender and number.

(6) افعال ناقصہ **Defective Verbs,** such as معلوم - ہونا - بننا - ہونا - نکلنا etc. require مبتدا Subject and خبر Predicate only and not the مبتدا Subject and مفعول Object like other Verbs, as مہابھر موتی کا کہنا جھوٹ ہوا - بہادر نکلا

(7) Sometimes خبر Predicate is omitted, as کریم مدرسہ میں ہے Karim is in the school Here 'حاضر present' is omitted. Sometimes مبتدا Subject, خبر Predicate and the sentence even is omitted, as, if any body ask '? تم میں سے کون ہوشیار ہے Who is clever among you ?' the answer shall be 'رام داس Ram Dass'; Predicate is omitted here. If ask 'کیا موہن ? ہوشیار ہے Is Mohan clever ?' and the answer be 'ہوشیار ہے' Subject is omitted here. If the answer is only 'ہاں Yes' the whole sentence is omitted.

(8) In Urdu مبتدا Subject comes first, next خبر Predicate and then کلمہ ربط Copula

(b)—جملہ فعلیہ **Jumla Feliya.**

(1) جملہ فعلیہ is that in which مسند الیہ Subject is اسم Noun and مسند Predicate a فعل Verb. In جملہ فعلیہ - مسند الیہ Subject is named Nominative and مسند Predicate فعل Verb.

(2) Like مبتدا Subject the Nominative is also either Noun or Predicate صفت Adjective without the thing qualified or شبهہ فعل Participle, as منگل آیا Mangal came. هم جاتے هیں We go. پرند اُڑ گیا The bird flew away. غریب مر جاتے هیں The poor die.

(3) There should be فعل Verb Transitive فاعل Nominative and as well as مفعول Objective, as چندرا نے پانی پیا Chandra drank water.

Some فعل Verbs have two Objects and some three.

(4) When the فاعل Nominative of a Passive Verb is not known its real مفعول Object is called مفعول فاعل نا معلوم Object without Nominative, as چیتا مارا گیا The tiger is killed. خط بهیجے گئے The letters are sent.

(5) Some فعل متعدي Transitive Verbs take two مفعول Objects. The first is called مفعول به Direct Object and the 2nd مفعول ثاني **Indirect Object**, as میں نے جواهر کو بهادر سمجها I thought Jawahir to be a hero.

(6) In Urdu فاعل Nominative comes first then مفعول Object and then Verb, as پرشوتم نے سبق یاد کیا Parshotam learnt the lesson.

(7) Sometimes فعل Verb, فاعل Nominative مفعول Object and the sentence is omitted in answering a question, as ? کیامحمود آ گیا Has Mahmud come? (ans.) آگیا has come. کون بھاگ گیا Who ran away ? (ans.) Ahmad, etc., etc.

(8) Sometimes for fear one word is spoken for the whole sentence, as چور چور thief thief ! سانپ سانپ snake snake !

B.—جملہ ملتفت Complex Sentence.

جملہ ملتفت A Complex Sentence is one that contains at least two clauses one of which is dependent upon the other, as میں اُس آدمی سے ملا جسنے مجھے گھوڑا بیچا تھا I met the man who sold me the horse. Here اصلی جملہ Principal Sentence is میں اُس آدمی سے ملا *I met the man* and the dependent or تابع جملہ Subordinate Sentence is جسنے مجھے گھوڑا بیچا تھا *who sold me the horse.*

تابع جملہ is called فقرہ Clause.

تابع جملے Subordinate Sentences are of three kinds:

(1) فقرہ اسم Noun Clause.

(2) فقرہ صفت Adjective Clause.

(3) فقرہ صلہ فعل Adverbial Clause.

(1) فقرہ اسم **Noun Clause** is that which serves the purpose of a Noun for the principal clause, as میرا فیصلہ یہہ ہے "کہ آدمی مجرم ہے" My judgment is *that the man is guilty*.

(2) فقرہ صفت **Adjective Clause** is that which may have relation of Adjective with a noun or noun-equivalent in the Principal Sentence, as وہ " جسکو تو پیار کرتاہے " بیمار ہے He *whom thou lovest* is sick.

(3) فقرہ صلہ فعل **Adverbial Clause** is that which may have relation with the Verb in the Principal Sentence, as وہ ایسا کمزور تھا "کہ وہ کھڑا نہ ہوسکا " He was so feeble *that he could not stand*.

C.—جملہ مرکب Compound Sentence.

جملہ مرکب A **Compound Sentence** consists of two or more sentences of *equal rank* and therefore called **Co-ordinate** joined together by a **Co-ordinate Conjunction.** مرکب جملے **Compound Sentences** are divided into three Classes :

(1) جملہ معطوفہ **Cumulative Sentence.**

(2) جملہ مستدرکہ **Adversative Sentence.**

(3) جملہمعللہ **Illative Sentence.**

(1) Where one clause is simply added to the other is called جملہ معطوفہ **Cumulative,** as لچھمن نے سواری کی اور جیمس پیدل چلا Lachhman rode and James walked.

(2) Where one clause is in opposition to the other it is called مستدرکہ **Adversative,** as وہ نہ آویگا پر اُسنے خبر بھیجی ہے He would not come, but he sent a message.

(3) Where one clause gives the علت Cause and the other معلول the Effect it is called معللہ **Illative,** as زور سے بارش ہوئی اس لئے ہم اندر چلے گئے It rained heavily, therefore we went indoors.

LESSONS FOR SENTENCE STUDY.

LESSON 1.

مت do not, don't. ستارے stars. تیز fast. غمگین sad. ڈرنا fear. چمکنا shine. آگ fire. دودھ milk. کہنا tell. کھٹا sour. جلنا burn. گرم hot. سچ truth. ڈھونا carry. دریا river. پلنگ - بسترہ bed. بوجھہ load. بہنا flow.

مت ڈر Do not (don't) fear. دریا بہتے ھیں Rivers flow. ستارے چمکتے ھیں Stars shine. اسکے پاس ایك چاقو ھے He has a knife.

آم کھٹا ھے The mango is sour. وہ غمگین ھے He is sad. اُونٹ بوجھہ ڈھوتے ھیں Camels carry loads. دودہ گرم ھے The milk is hot. گھر پر رہ Stop at home. وہ رکھتا ھے - اسکے پاس ھے He has. تیز چل Walk fast. آگ جلتی ھے Fire burns. میں رکھتا ھوں-میرے پاس ھے I have. پلنگ پر جاؤ Go to bed.

LESSON 2.

اب now. دور far. کیوں why. کہنا tell. منت کرنا beg. گھر house. بہت very. لانا bring. گرا fell. ساتھہ with. جلد soon. قلم pen. اچھا good. وھاں there. کنواں well. کاغذ paper. لینا take. کہا said. گیا went. ایسا so. کھڑا ھونا stand.

اب اسکے پاس جاؤ Go to him now.

تم میرے ساتھہ چلوگے ؟ Will you come with me ?

میں آپ سے منت کرتا ھوں I beg you.

تم وھاں کیوں جاتے ھو ؟ Why do you go there ?

دس لڑکے دوڑے Ten boys ran.

اُسنے ایسا کہا He said so.

ایك آدمی کنوے میں گرا A man fell in the well.

وہ بہت جلد جاویگي She will go very soon.

تم اچھے لڑکے نہیں ھو You are not a good boy.

وہ کنویں میں گر پڑا He fell in the well.

میرا قلم مت لو Do not take my pen.

وہ لکھنؤ گیا He went to Lucknow.

میں اُس پر کھڑا نہیں ھوسکتا I cannot stand on it.

اگر میں اُس سے کہوں تو وہ جائیگا He will go if I tell him.

میرا گھر دور ھے My house is far.

کاغذ و قلم لاؤ Bring pen and paper.

LESSON 3.

روپیہ پیسہ money. ھمشیرہ sister. پرانا old. حالانکہ though. جیب pocket. کتنا how much. پھاٹك gate. آج to-day. کپڑے clothes. نام name. زھر poison. تین بار three times. توڑ ڈالی broke. کیا what. مرجاتا ھے dies. جواب answer. بوتل bottle. بخوبی very well. باز آنا avoid. صحبت company. جاننا

know. سمجھنا understand. بیمار sick. عرصہ دراز long time. بات word. کل yesterday. شیریں sweet.

مطلق at all. زیادہ گرم hotter.

اُس نے روپیہ اپنی جیب میں رکھہ لیا He put the money in his pocket.

اُسنے بوتل توڑ ڈالی He broke the bottle.

میں تمہارے بھائی کو عرصہ دراز سے جانتا ہوں I know your brother for a long time.

یہہ میٹھے پھل تمہاری ہمشیرہ کے واسطے ہیں These sweet fruits are for your sister.

تمہاری گائے کتنا دودہ دیتی ہے How much milk does your cow give ?

آپکا اسم مبارک (یا اسم شریف) کیا ہے ? What is your name ?

میرا نام حیدر خاں ہے یا مجھے حیدر خاں کہتے ہیں My name is Hyder Khan.

میں آپکو بخوبی جانتا ہوں I know you very well.

تم میری بات مطلق نہیں سمجھتے You do not understand my words at all.

میرا مکان بہت پرانا ہے My house is very old.

کیا آپ بتا سکتے ھیں بادشاہ کی کیا عمر ھے ؟ Can you say how old the King is ?

پانچ آدمی اور دوعورتیں آرھی ھیں Five men and two women are coming.

پھاٹك میں تالالگادو Lock up the gate.

زھر کھانے سے آدمی مرجاتا ھے Man dies by eating poison.

بے وقوفوں کی صحبت سے باز رھو Avoid the company of fools.

اُس دن تم کہاں گئے تھے Where did you go on that day ?

کیا آپ میری لڑکی کو چنگا کرسکتے ھیں Can you cure my sick girl ?

آپ کے کتنے فرزند ھیں How many sons have you ?

کل آج کی بہ نسبت زیادہ گرم تھا Yesterday was hotter than to-day.

حالانکہ میں نے تین بار اُس سے پوچھا - اُسنے کوئی جواب نہیں دیا Though I asked him three times, he did not answer.

LESSON 4.

ھرروز every day. اس وقت at this time. غسل کرنا bathe. ابھی just now. بس کرنا stop. دل heart. طرف towards.

کھانا food. جان soul. سے since. کم less. پہونچنا reach. طبیعت - تندرستی health. معاملہ matter. پھول flower. شام evening. ھل چل agitation. سب سے خوبصورت loveliest. قیمت price. دنیا world. چھوڑدینا give up. نقصان loss. معاوضہ دینا recompense.

تم دو بجے کے بعد یہاں ھر روز کیوں آیا کرتے ھو ؟ Why do you come here every day after 2 o'clock ?

وہ ابھي دوکان کی طرف جاتے ھیں He is just now going towards the shop.

کل شام سے میری والدہ کي طبعیت بھي ٹھیك نہیں ھے Since yesterday evening my mother's health is not good.

اِس کتاب کی کیا قیمت ھے ؟ What is the price of this book ?

میرے پاس وقت اس وقت صرف پانچ روپئے ھیں There are only five rupees with me at this time.

اچھا اب بس کیجئے Well, please stop now.

بیچاري بوڑھی عورت کو کم کھانا ملتا ھے The poor old woman gets little food.

نہیں کیا ھوا ھے ؟ What is the matter with you ?

دنیا میں ھل چل مچی ھے There is agitation all over the world.

میں آج غسل نہ کرونگا ورنہ دیر ہوجائیگی I shall not bathe to-day otherwise I shall be late.

میں تمھیں دل و جان سے پیار کرتا ہوں I love you heart and soul.

آج میں وہاں کسی حالت سے نہیں پہونچ سکتا In any case I cannot reach there to-day.

لکھو تو میں دیکھوں تم کیسے لکھتے ہو Just write, let me see how you do it.

یہہ پھول سب سے خوبصورت ہے This flower is loveliest of all.

اپنے جیتے جی میں اُسے نہ چھوڑونگا I will not give it up as long as I live.

میں آپکے نقصان کا معاوضہ دینے کی کوشش کرونگا

I will try to recompense you for your loss.

LESSON 5.

تمام سرگذشت the whole story. مضرت harm. وسیع جنگل vast forest. بے کم و کاست without disguise. واضح رہے must know. فرسنگ league. نہایت متحیر ہوئی was very much surprised. قزاق highwayman. دیو giant. آخرکار at length.

کافی sufficient. خیمہ زن ہوئے encamped. علامت marks.
نزدیک in the neighbourhood. شفقت affection.
باوجود notwithstanding. تعمیل کی گئی executed.
پریشانی و گھبراہٹ Perplexity and jeopardy.
دعوی کرنا defy. اہل حرفہ mechanic. سموسے cream-tort.
تاجر merchant.

میرے بھائی نے تمام سرگذشت اُس سے بے کم و کاست کہہ سنائی My brother told him the whole story without disguise.

اُسکی ماں دیو کو دیکھکر نہایت متحیر ہوئی His mother was very much surprised to see the giant.

میں کافی علامت اپنی شفقت کی ظاہر نہیں کرسکتا I cannot give sufficient marks of my affection.

وزیر کے حکم کی فوراً تعمیل کی گئی The Vizier's orders were immediately executed.

میں دعوی کرتا ہوں کہ کوئی مجھسے بڑھکر سموسے نہیں بناسکتا I defy anyone to make a better cream-tort.

خبردار نہ اسکو ماریو اور نہ کسی طرحکی مضرت پہونچائیو Take care you do not beat him nor do him the least harm.

یہہ واضح رہے کہ اس گھر کا مالک ایک قزاق ہے You must know that the master of this house is a highwayman.

آخرکار ہم عدن پہونچے اور اس شہر کے نزدیک خیمہ‌زن ہوئے At length we arrived at Aden and encamped in the neighbourhood of that place.

لیکن باوجود پریشانی و گھبراہت کے بھی میں نے ہوشیاری سے اپنا دروازہ بند کرلیا But, notwithstanding the perplexity and jeopardy I was in I had the precaution to shut my door

دینا ناتھ اہل حرفہ نہیں ہے بلکہ تاجر ہے Dinanath is not a mechanic, but a merchant.

وہ مجھے اپنے پیچھے ہاتھی پر بٹھا کر ایک وسیع جنگل میں جوکہ شہر سے کئی فرسنگ پر تھا لے گیا He taking me behind him upon the elephant carried me to a vast forest some leagues from the town.

LESSON 6.

واپس آوینگے will return. سکھلاتا ہے teaches. سوتا ہوا sleeping. ہفتے weeks. فارسی Persian. شیر lion. لڑے fought. فروخت کرتی ہے sells. شکست ہوئی were defeated. بہت اچھا very good.

بهالو bear. قریب near. سے - نسبت بہ than. تالاب ank. بهیڑیا wolf. سر نامہ address. سوچنا think شخص person. سونا gold. عنایت kindness. غلطی پر هے is mistaken. آرام comfort. پرسوں day before yesterday. جگانا wake up.

میرے والد تین هفتے میں واپس آوینگے My father will return in three weeks.

سپاهی بڑی بہادری سے لڑے لیکن انکی شکست هوئی The soldiers fought with great bravery but they were defeated.

بهالو بهیڑئے کي بہ نسبت زیادہ طاقتورهوتاهے The bear is stronger than the wolf.

اگر کوئي آدمي یہہ سوچے کہ یہاں بہت سوناهے تو وہ غلطي پر هے If any man think there is much gold here, he is mistaken.

پرسوں سے میري همشیرہ کو کوئي فارسي نهیں پڑهاتا Since day before yesterday no one teaches Persian to my sister.

اُس تالاب کے قریب ایك عورت بہت اچهے پهل فروخت کرتي هے A girl sells very good fruits near that tank.

اُس شخص کا جو کل آپکے مکان پر آیا تھا کیا سرنامہ ھے ? What is the address of the person who had come to your bouse yesterday ?

آپکی عنایت سے میں نے وھاں بہت آرام پایا تھا By your kindness I had got much comfort there.

تم کھاتے تو میں بھي تمھارے ساتھہ کھاتا If you had eaten I too would have eaten with you.

سوتے ھوئے شیر کو مت جگاؤ Don't wake up a sleeping lion.

انھوں نے آپ سے یہہ بات کہي ھوگي پر مجھسے کسی نے نہیں کہا He might have told you this, but no one told me.

اگر بارش ھونے لگي تو میں وھاں نہ جا پاؤنگا If it begins to rain I shall not be able to go there.

LESSON 7.

اب تک still. پسند کرنا like. بہت many.
تصویر picture. تالي بجانا clapping hands.
غلطي mistake. تعریف کرتا تھا was admiring.
خوشي joy. چوري ھوئي تھیں were stolen. دکھلانا show.
ھنسا laughed. مل گئیں have been found. توڑڈالا broke.
زور سے loudly. ایسي such. جلادیا burnt.

فرخت هونے کو to be sold. سستي cheap. کھیت field. حکم ماننا obey. قیمت value. اُتار ڈالنا take off. خواہ whether. جہالت ignorance. مسجد mosque. چہار طرف round.

اگر تمہارے پاس وہ تصویر جسکي میں تعریف کرتا تھا اب تک ہے تو انہیں دکھلاؤ If you have still the picture which I was admiring, show it to him.

اسنے تختی توڑڈالي کاپیاں پھاڑ ڈالیں اور تصویریں جلا دیں He broke the slate, tore the copies and burnt the picture.

تم میرا حکم مانوگے خواہ پسند کرو یا نہ کرو You shall obey me, whether you like it or not.

خوشی کے مارے تالی پیٹ کر لڑکا زور سے ھنسا Clapping its hands for joy, the child laughed loudly.

گھوڑے جو بکاؤ ھیں کم قیمت کے ھیں The horses which are to be sold are of little value.

جہالت یا غفلت کے باعث یہہ غلطی ہوئی Ignorance or negligence has caused this mistake.

جو کتابیں چوری گئی تھیں مل گئیں The books that were stolen have been found.

ایسی کتاب ایک شلنگ میں سستي ھے Such a book as this is cheap at a shilling.

آجکل غلہ سستا نہیں ہے Now-a-days corn is not cheap.

مسجد میں جانے سے پیشتر جوتے اُتارو Take off your shoes before you go into the mosque.

مکان کے چہار طرف بہت سے درخت ہیں Round the house there are many trees.

آدمي عورتیں کھیت میں کیا کررہے ہیں What are the men and women doing in this field ?

LESSON 8.

جگہہ place. بخار fever. مزے اُڑانا enjoy. بڑا large. دوا medicine. صبر patience. شہر city. سمندر کا کنارہ seashore. ورزش exercise. ٹھہرنا stay. از راہ نوازش please. طاقتور strong. بھي too. معاف کرنا forgive. گھومنا walking. کھڑے ہیں are standing. خطا offence. صاف pure. فسادي quarrelsome. ہوا air. خوش glad. تندرست healthy. ناراض ہونا getting angry.

بمبئي کس قسم کي جگہہ ہے What kind of place is Bombay ?

بمبئي سمندر کے کنارے پر ایک بڑا شہر ہے Bombay is a large city at the seashore.

از راہ نوازش میري خطا معاف کر دیجئے Please forgive my offence.

چند دنوں سے میري طبیعت کچھہ خراب هے For the last few days my health has been a little bad.

وے فسادي آدمی هیں They are quarrelsome men.

میں بڑا خوش هونگا اگرتم میرے پاس رهو I shall be very glad if you live with me.

اگر تمکو تپ هوتا هے تو کوئی دوا کهاؤ If you have fever use some medicine.

خوب ورزش کیا کرو تاکہ طاقتور هو Take good exercise so that you become strong.

هر روز علی‌الصباح صاف هوا میں گهومنے سے تندرستی قائم رهتی هے Walking every morning in pure air makes one healthy.

آپ کیا کرنے چاهتے هیں What do you want to do ?

آپ اتنے ناراض کیوں هوتے هیں Why are you getting so angry ?

تم کو کیا هے تم بیٹهے مزے اڑاؤ What does it matter to you, sit and enjoy yourself.

ذرا صبر کرو Have a little patience.

ٹهہرو میں بهی تمهارے ساتهہ چلونگا Stay, I too shall come with you.

هم کهڑے هیں تم جلدی سے آؤ We are standing, you come soon.

LESSON 9.

پہلا first. اتوار Sunday. گوریا sparrow. هیرا diamond. موسم گرما summer. پانی پیدا taking a drink. آرام کرنا rest. سایه shade. چشمه fountain. تکیه pillow. گرمی heat. بڑے older. اُٹھاے رکھتا هے raises. ایندهن fuel. چهوٹے younger. سر head. خوبصورت beautiful. بهینس buffaloes. گردن neck. هر ایک چیز everything. چمچمانا twinkle. بڑهنا growing. نظر آتی هے looks. آسمان sky. اُڑنا fly.

هفته کا پہلادن کیا هوتاهے ? What is the first day of the week ?

هفته کا پہلا دن اتوار هوتا هے The first day of the week is Sunday.

موسم گرما میں درختوں کا سایه همکو آفتاب کی گرمی سے بچاتا هے In summer the shade of the trees saves us from the heat of the sun.

درخت اکثر ایندهن کے کام بهی آتے هیں Trees are often used as fuel also.

بارش کے بعد هر ایک چیز کیسی خوبصورت نظر آتی هے How beautiful everything looks after the rains !

پرندوں کے بازو هوتے هیں اور وے اُنسے اُڑتے هیں The birds have wings and they fly with them.

ایک گوریا چشمہ میں پانی پی رہی ھے A sparrow is taking a drink at the fountain.

میرے دو بھائي مجھہ سے بڑے ھیں اور دو چھوٹے ھیں Two of my brothers are older than I and one is younger.

میرے والد کے پاس کچھہ کھیت ھیں اور بہت سی بھینس ھیں My father has some fields and a good many buffaloes.

ستارے آسمان میں ھیرے کي مانند چمچماتے ھیں Stars twinkle in the sky like a diamond.

اگر ھم چھوٹا تکیہ استعمال کریں تو زیادہ آرام ملیگا We shall rest better if we use a small pillow.

بڑا تکیہ سر کو زیادہ اٹھاے رکھتا ھے اور ھماري گردن کو بڑھنے سے روکتا ھے A big pillow raises the head too much and keeps our neck from growing.

LESSON 10.

اُسنے اپنے قول کو پورا کیا He kept his word. اُسنے انھیں ایک بڑی رقم قرض میں دی He lent them a large sum of money.

جگنو اندھیرے میں چمکتے ھیں Fireflies shine in the darkness.

اس پر دھوپ کا اثر نہیں پڑتا He is proof against the sun.

اُسکے آتے ھی میں بھاگا No sooner he had arrived than I fled.

ہم پہلے بھي ملے We have met before. اُسنے فوراً مجھے پہچانا He recognised me at once. ميں ايک دم بمبئي جاؤنگا I will go straight to Bombay. ميں نے پيٹ بھر کھايا I did full justice to the dinner. آپکے آنے سے ميں بہت خوش ہوں I am very pleased at your coming. تھوڑے آدمي ھيں جو ايسا کرسکتے ھيں There are a few men who can do so. کوئي کوئي لوگ کہتے ھيں کہ وہ فرار ھو گيا Some say that he has absconded. ميري صلاح مانو Hear my advice. مجھے يہاں آے ہوے ايک گھنٹہ کے قريب ھوا I have been here nearly an hour. وے جنگل ميں کام کرتے ھيں They work in woods. يہہ ايک دلچسپ قصہ ھے It is an interesting story. وہ ايماندار سمجھا جاتا ھے He is believed to be honest. اُنہوں نے دشمن کے جہاز کو ڈبو ديا They sank the enemy's ship. فقير نے دعا کي کہ خدا مجھے برکت دے The beggar prayed that God might bless me. وصيت لکھنے کے لئے اکثر وکيل بلايا جاتا ھے A lawyer is often called in to write a man's will. وہ چھاتي ميں درد کي شکايت کرتا ھے He complains of a pain in the chest. مصيبت کے وقت دوست اکثر کنارہ کش ھو جاتے ھيں Friends frequently fall off in adversity. وہ اپنی تنخواہ ھر ماہ سے ۲۰ روپيہ جمع کرتا ھے Every month he lays by 20 rupees from his pay.

LESSON 11.

ميں آگرہ ميں تاج محل کي شان ديکھکر حيرت ميں پڑ گيا I was astonished at the grandeur of the Taj Mahal at Agra. معلوم ديتا ھے کہ ترکي سلطنت زوال پر ھے It seems that the Turkish power is on the decline. ھم نے کسي کو بولتے سنا ليکن يہہ نہ سنا کہ اُسنے کيا کہا We heard some one speaking but we did not listen to what he said. اس کتاب کے طبع جديد کے پہلے حصہ

میں بہت کچھہ اضافہ کیا گیا ھے In the new edition of that book a large addition has been made to the first part of it. بغیر محنت کے عظمت حاصل نہیں ھوتی No one attains greatness without labour. فطرت میں ھر ایک چیز خدا کی نیکی کا اشتہار دیتی ھے Everything in nature proclaims the goodness of God. ھم ادنی جانوروں سے بہت سے مفید سبق سیکھہ سکتے ھیں We may derive many useful lessons from the lower animals. پرھیزگاری سے تندرستی محفوظ رھتی ھے Temperance preserves our health. بادشاہ نے اسکو جلاوطن کر دیا He was banished from the country by the king. اسکے مالک نے اُسکا قصور معاف کر دیا His master forgave him his fault. کیا سب موت کی نیند سو رھینگے ? Must all sleep the sleep of death ? کیا تاج محل ایک عالیشان عمارت نہیں ھے ? Is not the Taj Mahal a magnificent building? بھیڑیا کتے کے خاندان کا ھے The wolf belongs to the dog family. سب آدمی زیادہ عرصہ تک جینے کی اُمید رکھتے ھیں All men hope to live a long life. اسنے سب سوالوں کے صحیح جواب دیئے He answered all the questions correctly. ھماری اُمیدیں اکثر باطل ھو جاتی ھیں Our hopes are often frustrated. تم بے وقوف تھے جو تم نے ایسا خیال کیا You were a fool to think so.

LESSON 12.

اگر میں وھاں ھوتا تو تمھیں روپیہ دیتا Were I there I would pay the money.

اگر وہ مجھہ سے ملے تو وہ مجھے فوراً پہچان لیگا If he should meet me he would recognize me at once.

گانا خوش گوار معلوم ھوتا ھے To sing is pleasant.

آپ جاوینگے یا ٹھہرینگے Will you go or will you stay ?

ہم راستہ نہیں جانتے We do not know the way.

دوڑنا صحت بخش ورزش ہے Running is healthy exercise.

میں سواری کا شوقین ہوں I am fond of riding.

کیا تم اپنے ہاتھ صابن سے دھوتے ہو Do you wash your hands with soap ?

کیا تم سمجھتے ہو کاشی ناتھ اُس عہدہ کے لایق ہے Do you think Kashi Nath is fit for that post ?

میری نبض بخار کے باعث جلدی جلدی چل رہی ہے My pulse is quick with fever.

جب میں باہر گھومنے جاتا ہوں تو ہاتھ میں ہمیشہ چھڑی لئے رہتا ہوں I always take a stick in my hand when I go out for a walk.

آجکل تمہاری آمدنی کیا ہے ? What is your income now-a-days ?

میں چار مہینہ سے بیمار ہوں I have been ill for four months.

ہاے آج میرے بڑے بیٹے کا انتقال ہو گیا Alas ! my eldest son died to-day.

اب آپ مجھے بتائیے آپکی کیا مرضی ہے Now tell me what is your desire.

میرے والد آہستہ آہستہ سڑک پر آرہے ہیں My father is coming slowly along the road.

اس کتاب میں کتنے صفحے ہیں ? How many pages are there in this book ?

LESSON 13.

چرندوں و پرندوں کي بولي

Speech of Beasts and Birds.

کتا بھوکتا ھے The dog *barks*.

بلي گھر گھر یا میوں میوں کرتی ھے The cat *purs* or *mews*.

گھوڑا ھنہناتا ھے The horse *neighs*.

گائے رمبھاتي ھے The cow *lows*.

سانڈ ڈکرانا ھے The bull *bellows*.

بھیڑ ممیاتي ھے The sheep *bleats*.

سیار ھوا ھوا کرتا ھے The jackal *howls*.

شیر گرجتا ھے The lion *roars*.

چیتا غراتا ھے The tiger *growls*.

اونٹ بلبلاتا ھے The camel *grunts*.

ھاتھي چنگھاڑتا ھے The elephant *trumpets*.

بندر چچیاتا ھے The monkey *chatters*.

مور کوکتا ھے The peacock *screams*.

مرغ بانگ دیتا ھے The cock *crows*.

گوریا چیں چیں کرتي ھے The sparrow *chirps*.

الو ھو ھو کرتا ھے The owl *hoots*.

سانپ پھپکارتا ھے The serpent *hisses*.

شہد کی مکھی بھنبھناتي ھے The bee *hums*.

LESSON 14.

سوالیہ جملے Interrogatory Sentences.

کیا تم یہہ کام کرسکتے هو Can you do this work ?

تم نے کچھہ سنا هے Have you heard something ?

تم کیا کر رهے هو What are you doing ?

کیا تم نے اُسے مارا تھا Had you beaten him ?

کیا تم نے اُسے پیسے دئے تھے Did you give her pice ?

وهاں کون هے Who is there ?

تم کیسے هو How are you ?

تم کہاں جاتے هو Where do you go ?

وہ کہاں تھا Where was he ?

کیا میں جاسکتا هوں Can I go ?

کیا وہ یہاں هے Is he here ?

کیا وے جارهے هیں Are they going ?

کیا وہ سو رها هے Is he sleeping ?

وہ کہاں گیا تھا Where did he go to ?

وہ کسکي بہو هے Whose daughter-in-law is she ?

وہ یہاں کیوں آیا تھا Why was he here ?

تمہارا علاج کون کرتاهے Whose treatment you are under ?

کیا تم بہرے هو Are you deaf ?

میں اُس کے واسطے کیا کرسکتا ھوں What can I do for her ?

بچہ موت کي بابت کیا جانے What does a child know of death ?

کیا اسکي شادی ھوگئي ھے Is he married ?

کیا ایك خط بھی نہ ڈال سکے Could not you drop a letter even ?

کیا تم گھر جانا چاھتے ھو Do you like to go home ?

تم کسکے بیٹے ھو Whose son are you ?

کیا تم کلکتہ جا رھے ھو Are you going to Calcutta ?

کیا تم گھر جاؤگے Will you go home ?

تمہارا گھر کونسا ھے Which is your house ?

LESSON 15.

امریہ (حکمي) جملے

Imperative Sentences.

[*Note.*—'تو thou' is understood before Verbs, as. کھا eat, تو کھا eat thou, پڑہ read, تو پڑہ read thou, تم جاؤ you go, تم پڑھو you read.]

یہاں آؤ Come here. وھاں جاؤ Go there.

میرا قلم مت لو Do not take my pen.

یہہ کرو Do this.

دروازہ بند کرو Shut the door.

اپنا منھہ دھو Wash your face.

مت سو Don't sleep.

(تو) چپ رہ Be silent (thou)

لوٹ آؤ Come back.

مجھے دو Give me.

آمدنی سے زیادہ خرچ مت کرو Keep your expenses within your income.

دوسروں کو گالی مت دو Do not abuse others.

کبھی جھوٹ نہ بولو Never tell a lie.

اسے وہاں رکھو Put it there.

خدا سے دعا کرو Pray to God.

جلدی کرو Make haste.

دودھ پیو Drink the milk.

اپنے بھائی سے پوچھو Ask your brother.

(تو) اٹھہ Get up (thou).

بیٹھہ جاؤ Sit down.

(تو) کھڑا هو Stand (thou).

اپنے والدین کی عزت کرو Honour your parents.

اسے خوب یاد رکھو Remember this well.

جو برا هے اس سے نفرت کرو اور جو اچھا هے اسے پیار کرو Hate that which is evil, love that which is good.

CHAPTER X.

LESSON 1.

Idiomatic Use of Verbs.

آپ کیوں اتني ڈبنگ اُڑا رھے ھو Why are you boasting so much?

میں نے سیکڑوں روپئے پھونک دئے I squandered hundreds of rupees.

میں نے اسے خوب آڑے ھاتھہ لیا I took him well to task.

تمھارے مارے ناکوں میں دم آگیا I have become sick of you.

آجکل کانگریس زور پکڑ رھي ھے The Congress is gaining ground now-a-days.

اسے دیکھکر میرا دل پگھل گیا My heart sank when I saw him.

شیر کو مارنا میرے بائیں ھاتھہ کا کھیل ھے It is light work for me to kill a lion.

وہ گھر میں بیٹھا مکھي مار رھا ھے He is idling at home.

اسنے بھري تھالي میں لات مار دي He fought with his bread and butter.

میں نے اسکے دانت کھٹے کر دئے I set their teeth on edge.

تمھاری بات میرے دل میں لگ گئي Your words cut me to the heart.

آپ نے اچھي پھبتي کہي You cut the joke well.

وہ بیچارا ریوڑي کے پھیر میں پڑا ھے The poor fellow is involved in difficulties.

وہ دال روٹي سے خوش ھے He is well off.

میں نے دن کو دن اور رات کو رات نہ سمجھا I was totally absorbed in nursing her.

اسنے اسکو منھہ توڑ جواب دیا He silenced him.

اسکی چھاتی پر سانپ لوٹتا ہے He burns with jealousy.

جب میں نے اُسے دیکھہ لیا تب جی میں جی آیا On seeing him I was comforted.

LESSON 2.

Phrases formed of Verbs.

روکھے پن سے دیکھنا to look cool upon.

جھاڑو پھیرنا to make a clean sweep of.

کان بھرنا to poison one's ear.

موقع ہاتھہ لگنا to stand a good chance.

ہاتھہ پاؤں مارنا to strain every nerve.

بڑا بول بولنا to talk big.

Phrases formed of other Parts of Speech.

موٹی غلطی gross error.

صورت حرام fair without and foul within.

لڑائی کی جڑ apple of discord, bone of contention.

خیالی پلاؤ fumes of fancy.

بھاؤ کے بھاؤ at par.

گھاٹے پر below par.

نشے میں چور dead drunk.

Some idiomatic forms by adding اُڑانا - سمجھانا - جھیلنا - دینا - اُٹھانا - کھونا, etc. to different nouns, as :

دکھہ اُٹھانا to take pains.

مزے اُڑانا to enjoy oneself.

دماغ لڑانا to rack the brain.

قسم کھانا to take an oath.

غصہ میں آنا to get angry.
مصیبت جھیلنا to suffer calamity.
گپ اُڑانا to gossip.
ہوا کھانا to walk.
ہوش اُڑ جانا to become perplexed.
مال اُڑانا to eat delicious dishes.

LESSON 3.

Repetition of Words.

Some expressions are made by the repetition of Noun, Pronoun, Adjective, Adverb, Participle and Verb.

(1) *Repetition of Noun ;*

گھر گھر house to house.
گاؤں گاؤں village to village.
پیڑ ہی پیڑ trees and trees alone.
آن کی آن میں in a moment.
روز بروز day by day.
درجہ بدرجہ degree by degree.
در در door to door.
جھنڈ کے جھنڈ swarms after swarms.
شہر شہر city to city.
سال بسال every year.
قدم بقدم step by step.

(2) *Pronoun :*

سب کے سب all.
کوئی نہ کوئی someone.

آپ سے آپ itself, himself.

(3) *Adjective :*

گورے گورے fair ones.
میٹھے میٹھے sweet ones.
موٹے موٹے fat ones.
بڑے بڑے big ones.
کم از کم at least.
کالے کالے black ones.
اچھے اچھے good ones.
کچھ نہ کچھ something or other
چھوٹے چھوٹے small ones.
زیادہ سے زیادہ at most.

دبلے پتلے thin and lean.

(4) *Adverb :*

جہاں کہیں wherever. کبھی کبھی sometimes.
جیسے تیسے somehow. جب کبھی whenever.
ادھر اودھر hither and thither. تیوں تیوں...جیوں جیوں as...as.
رفتہ رفتہ by and by. تہاں تہاں...جہاں جہاں whereso-ever..there.
آہستہ آہستہ slowly.
کہاں کہاں in what places.

(5) *Participle :*

ہنستے ہنستے by laughing (too much). جاتے جاتے by going (regularly)
روتے روتے by weeping.
پڑھتے پڑھتے by reading (continuously). بلاتے بلاتے by calling (many many times).
کھاتے کھاتے eating (the same thing daily).

LESSON 4.

Antonyms or Opposite Words.

جمع کرنا add-منہا کرنا subtract بنانا build-ڈھانا raze.
عمر رسیدہ aged-جوان young. قدیم ancient-جدید modern.
قرض لینا borrow-قرض دینا lend. بہادری bravery-بزدلی cowardice
صاف clear-میلا dirty. بے رحم cruel-مہربان kind.
گراں dear-ارزاں cheap. دانا wise-نادان foolish.
آسان easy-مشکل difficult. کبھی ever-کبھی نہیں never.
کفایت شعاری frugality-فضول خرچی prodigality. بھرا ہوا full-خالی empty.
سابق former-بعد کا latter.
امید hope-ناامیدی despair. معصوم innocent-قصوروار guilty
زیادہ much-تھوڑا little. صلح peace-جنگ war.

کثرت plenty-قلت scarcity.	غرور pride-انکساری humility.
تیز quick-دھیما slow.	شاذ و نادر rarely-اکثر often.
چکنا smooth-کھردرا rough.	نرم soft-سخت hard.
شیریں sweet-تلخ bitter.	چوٹی top-تلی bottom.

LESSON 5.

Prefixes and Suffixes.

Prefixes.

از—from, than, by, of, with, as ; از بس—nevertheless, notwithstanding. از بر—by rote, by heart. از حد—boundless, infinite. از خود—voluntarily. از راہ—by the way of, *apropos*. از سر نو—newly, afresh, *de novo*, etc.

ال—the, as : الامان—for pity's sake ! Mercy ! البتہ (albatta)—certainly, positively. التوکل (altawakkul)—hypothetically. الحمد للہ (alhamdo-lillah)—God be praised. العبد (al'abd)—signature. الغرض (algaraz)—briefly, in short. القصہ (alqissa)—in a word. الوداع (alwidá,)—the last Friday of Ramzan, etc.

اہل—people, inhabitant, proprietor, citizen. اہل اللہ (ahl-i-Allah)—people of God. اہل حرفہ (ahl-i-hirfa)—artisans. اہل خرد (ahl-i-ḵhirad)—wise men. اہل علم (ahl-i-'ilm)—erudite, etc.

بہ-ب—with, by, for, from, in, to, on, as: بہ شوق (ba shauq)—delightfully بہ ہر صورت (ba har súrat)—by every means. بجاے (bajái)—in place of. بحدیکہ (bahadde ki)—to such a degree that, etc.

با—by, with, possessed of, as: باآبرو (bá-ábru)—respectably. با اتفاق (bá-ittifaq)—unanimously. با ادب (bá-adab)—polite, with good manners. با حیا (bá-hayá)—modest. با قرینه (bá-qarína)—in order. با مروت (bá-murawwat)—humane, kind. با وجود (bá-wajud)—notwithstanding. با وفا (bá-wafá)—true, faithful.

بال-بل—meaning: with, by, as; بالاتفاق (bil-ittifaq)—by chance. بالجبر (bil-jabr)—forcibly. بالذات (bil-zát)—naturally. بالضرور (bil-zarur)—necessarily. بالفرض (bil-farz)—supposing. بالفعل (bil-f'el)—now, at present. بالکل (bil-kul)—entirely. etc., etc.

بد—bad; wicked; mischievous, as: بد اختر (bad-akhtar)—ill-starred, unlucky. بد اخلاق (bad-ikhláq)—ill-mannered. بد اعمالی (bad-a'máli)—misdeeds. بد انتظامی (bad-intizámí)—maladministration, etc.

بر—up, above, at, in, with, forth, against. برآنا (bar-áná)—to be accomplished. بر خلاف - بر عکس (bar-'aks, bar-khiláf—on the contrary. بر محل-بر وقت (bar-mahal, bar-waqt)—opportune, seasonable. برلانا (bar-láná)—to fulfil etc.

بلا—without, as: بلا تردد (bilá taraddud)—without hesitation. بلا توقف (bilá tawaqquf)—without delay. بلا شک (bilá-shak)—doubtless. بلا ناغه (bilá nágá)—regularly. بلا وجه (bilá wajah)—without grounds, etc.

بے—without. as ; بے ادب (be-adab)—ill-behaved. بے ادبی (be-adabí)—incivility. بے اعتبار (be-e'tbár)—incredulous. بے انتہا (be-intihá)—endless. بے انصافی (be-insáfi)—injustice. بے ایمان (be-ímán)—infidel, dishonest, etc.

بیت—a house, temple, abode, as: بیت الحرام (bait-ul-hirám—the temple of Mecca. بیت الخلا (beit-ul-khalá—a necessary or privy. بیت الصنم (bait-ul-sanam)—an idol temple. بیت المال (bait-ul-mál)—the public treasury. بیت المقدس (bait-ul-muqaddas)—the Temple of Jerusalem.

پاے—foot, leg, foundation, as; پاے تخت (páetakht) royal residence, capital. پاے رکاب (páerikáb)—retinue. پاے مال کرنا (páemál karná)—to destroy. پایدار (páedár) firm, steady.

پُر—full, complete, abounding in, quite, as: پر تکلف (pur-takalluf)—ceremonious. پر خطر (pur-khatar)—very hazardous or risky. پر درد (pur-dard)—painful. پر سوز (pur-soz)—blazing. پر نور (pur-núr)—enlightened, etc.

پس—after, as: پس انداز—savings. پس پا کرنا—to repulse, to drive back. پس خوردہ—leavings, offal. پس غیبت—in one's absence. پس ماندہ—remaining, survivor, etc.

پیش—before, front, as: پیش ازیں—before this. پیش اندیش—prudent. پیشبندی—foresight. پیشقدمی—stepping before, leadership, etc.

تا—to, until, as far as, as long as, since, as : تازیست—while life remains. تابمقدور—to the utmost of one's ability. تاہم—yet, etc.

نا—negative, as : ناخوش—displeased. ناممکن—impossible. نادان—ignorant.

لا—absence, as : لاپتا—traceless. لاپروا—careless. لاچار—helpless. لاعلاج—having no remedy. لامذہب—irreligious, etc.

خوش—pleasing, as : خوشبو—good smell. خوشخط—good handwriting. خوش مزاج happy mood, etc.

سر—as : سرپرست—patron. سرگروہ—leader. سردار—chief. سرانجام—management. سرفراز—honoured, exalted. سرچشمہ—spring. سرحد boundaries, etc.

فی ال—as : فی الحال—at present. فی الجملہ—upon the whole. فی الواقع—in fact. فی الفور—immediately. خالبد یہہ—spontaneously. etc.

من—from, of, out of, on, as : من جانب—from the side of. منجملہ—in all. من بعد—hereafter, etc.

LESSON 6.

Suffixes.

گر—as : زرگر—goldsmith. قلعئی گر—gilder. کاریگر—workman. جادوگر—magician, etc.

خانہ—house, as : مسافر خانہ—traveller's house, inn. دواخانہ—dispensary. شفاخانہ—hospital. کتب خانہ—

library. کبوتر خانہ—pigeon-hole. عبادت خانہ—worship-house, temple, etc.

بان—as : گاڑیبان—cartman. شتربان—camel-driver. گلہ‌بان—pastor. نگہبان—guard, etc.

والا—as : پیسے والا—moneyed man. پانی والا—waterman. چکی والا—miller. دودھ والا—milkman, etc.

ی—as : لالچی—greedy. جنگلی—wild. معافی—pardon. غلطی—mistake. پیری—old age, etc.

دار—as : سمجھدار—intelligent. مالدار—wealthy. خبردار—careful. تھانہ‌دار—police inspector. رشتیدار—relative. چوکیدار—watchman. ٹھیکیدار—contractor. ایماندار—honest. خاردار—thorny. شاندار—magnificent, etc.

مند—as : فائدہ‌مند—profitable. حاجتمند—needy. عقلمند—wise. برومند—blessed. دولتمند—wealthy. ہنرمند—skilful. حوصلہ‌مند—ambitious, etc.

لا—as : زہریلا—poisonous. چمکیلا—bright. بھڑکیلا—splendid. گٹھیلا—knotty. کٹیلا—thorny. مٹیلا—dusty. نشیلا—intoxicating.

بخش—as : صحت بخش—healthgiving. طاقت بخش invigorating, etc.

ناک—خطرناک—perilous. غمناک—sorrowful. دہشتناک—frightful. دردناک—painful. شرمناک—shameful.

گاہ—place, as ; خوابگاہ—sleeping room. آرامگاہ—resting place. چراگاہ—meadow. عبادتگاہ—place of worship.

زدہ—struck, as : حیرت زدہ—wonder-struck. برق زدہ—thunder-struck. آفت زدہ—oppressed by adversity. قحط زدہ—famine-stricken. غم زدہ—sorrow-stricken, etc.

یافتہ—as : تعلیم یافتہ—educated. تربیت یافتہ—trained. سند یافتہ—certificated. عزت یافتہ—honoured.

آنہ—as : برادرانہ—brotherly. غریبانہ—poorly. امیرانہ—richly. جاہلانہ—like ignorant. شریفانہ—nobly. شاہانہ—kingly. دوستانہ—friendly. عاشقانہ—amorously.

باز—as : دغاباز—swindler, traitor. آتش باز—an exhibitor of fireworks. جلدباز—hasty, precipitate. قلاباز—one who takes a somersault. کبوتر باز—pigeon-flier.

LESSON 7.

Some Proverbial Expressions.

روپیہ کی ڈھال ڈال دے ربال A bribe in the lap blinds one's eyes.

ایک ترکش کی تیر ھیں } A chip of the old block.
ایک تورے کي روٹي کیا چھوٹي کیا موٹي }

ڈوبتے کو تنکے کا سہارا - مرتا کیا نہ کرتا A drowning man will catch at a straw.

میاں - صاحب سلامت دور کي اچھي A distant acquaintance is best.

ناچ نہ جانے آنگن ٹیڑھا A bad workman quarrels with his tools.

عقل علم کي کنجي هے Experience is the mother of science (wisdom ; knowledge).

کل کرتے آج کر آج کرتے اب Do not put off till to-morrow what you can to-day.

جیسا اپنے ساتهه چاهو ویسا اوروں کے ساتهه کرو Do to others as you wish done to you.

قضا کے آگے حکیم احمق • ڈوبی کي بوٹي بتادو حکیم جی Death defies the doctor.

مهنگا روئے ایک بار سستا روئے بار بار Dear is cheap and cheap is dear.

حسن دو دن کا مهمان هے Beauty is but a blossom

اُدهار کهانے سے بهوکا پڑا رهنا بهتر هے Better go to bed supper-less than rise in debt.

سارا جاتا دیکهئے آدها دیجیئے بانٹ Better give the wool than the whole sheep.

ساری نهیں تو آدهی سهي Half a loaf is better than no bread.

سفید بال موت کا پیغام Grey hairs are death's blossoms.

LESSON 8.

Some words having تنوین Tanwin.

اتفاقاً accidentally

دفعتاً suddenly

مثلاً for example, as

عموماً generally

قصداً intentionally

اصالتاً originally ; in person

حقارتاً contemptuously

امتحاناً by way of trial

خصوصاً particularly

سهواً erroneously

etc., etc.

LESSON 9.

Some words having sign of اضافت (زیر) sign of Possessive.

قادرِ مطلق Almighty

دستِ شفقت gracious hand

لباسِ فاخرہ precious dress

دستِ غربت poverty

دلِ ناپاک impure heart

تپِ دق pulmonary consumption, hectic fever

شیرِ دل lion-hearted

بسترِ مرگ death-bed

آبِ سرد cold water

افسرِ اعلیٰ superior officer

انگشتِ نر thumb

فہرستِ مضامین list of subjects

تپِ لرزہ an ague

یارِ غار bosom friend

اہلِ ہند inhabitants of India

ہمتِ مرداں courage of men

راحتِ دل peace of mind

etc. etc.

PART IV.

CHAPTER XI.

انشاء COMPOSITION.

[Conversation, Dialogue, Fables, Essays, Letter-writing, etc.]

Conversation.

(1)

کل جب میں تمہارے گھر تم سے ملنے گیا تھا تب تم کہاں گئے تھے ?
Where had you gone to when I went to your house to meet you yesterday

میں کہیں نہیں گیا تھا ۔ گھر میں تھا پر سویا ہوا تھا I had not gone anywhere, I was in the house but I was in bed at that time.

میں اُن صاحب کا پتہ پوچھنے آیا تھا جو کل تمہارے گھر پر آئے تھے
I had come to ask you the address of that gentleman who had come to your place yesterday.

میں نے اُن صاحب کو پیشتر کبھی نہیں دیکھا تھا اس لئے میں اُنکا پتہ نہیں جانتا I had never seen that gentleman before therefore I don't know his address.

میں سوچتا ہوں تمہارے والد ضرور جانتے ہونگے I think your father must be knowing his address.

ہاں وہ جانتے ہونگے انسے پوچھئے Yes, he might be knowing, ask him.

والد کہاں ہیں Where is he ?

وہ اپنے دفتر میں بیٹھے ہیں He is sitting in his office.

اچھا تو میں انکے پاس جاتا ہوں All right, then. I am going to him.

(2)

کیا تم نے کبھی طیارہ (ایرپلین) یا ہوائی جہاز دیکھا ہے؟ Have you ever seen an aeroplane?

ہاں میں نے ایک دن دیکھا تھا Yes, I saw it the other day.

وہ کہاں تھا Where was it?

وہ ہوا میں تھا It was in the air?

وہ کیا کر رہا تھا What was it doing?

وہ اُڑ رہا تھا It was flying.

طیارہ (ایرپلین) کو کون چلاتا ہے Who guides the aeroplane?

پائلٹ ایرپلین کو چلاتا ہے The pilot guides the aeroplane.

کیا تم طیارہ (ایرپلین) کے کل پرزے جانتے ہو Do you know the parts of an aeroplane?

ہاں ایک (propeller) دم - بازو اور پہیئے ہوتے ہیں Yes, it has a propeller, a tail, wings and wheels.

طیارہ (ایرپلین) میں پہیئے کیوں ہوتے ہیں Why does the aeroplane have wheels?

ہوا میں اُڑنے سے پہلے ایرپلین پہیوں کے ذریعہ سے زمین پر دوڑتا ہے اور جب زمین پر اُترتا ہے تب بھی پہئے استعمال ہوتے ہیں With the wheels the aeroplane runs along the ground before it flies up into the air. It also uses the wheels when it comes down to the ground.

طیارہ (ایرپلین) کس قدر تیز اُڑسکتا ہے How fast can an aeroplane fly?

وہ پرند سے زیادہ تیز اُڑتا ہے It flies faster than any bird.
ایرپلین کس کام میں آتے ہیں ؟ What are aeroplanes used for ?
ایرپلین لوگوں کو لے جاتے ہیں - خط اور پارسل لے جاتے ہیں - اور
لڑائی میں استعمال ہوتے ہیں Aeroplanes carry people. Aeroplanes carry letters and parcels. They are used in war.

Dialogue.

(1)

موتی—تم کہاں رہتے ہو - جواہر ؟

Moti—Where do you live, Jawahir ?

جواہر—میں ایک گاؤں میں رہتا ہوں جو یہاں سے دور نہیں ہے -

Jawahir—I live in a village not very far from here.

موتی—اپنے گاؤں کا راستہ بتا سکتے ہو ؟

Moti—Can you tell me the way to your village ?

جواہر—ہاں - بتا سکتا ہوں - تم قریب ڈیڑھ میل کے سڑک سے چلے جاؤ -
تب ایک چھوٹی سڑک پر بائیں جانب گھوم جاؤ - وہ چھوٹی سڑک - سیدھی
میرے گاؤں میں پہونچادیگی - وہیں رہتا ہوں - وہاں میرا مکان ہے -

Jawahir—Yes, I can. You go down the road about a mile and a half, and then turn to the left, along a small road. That small road will take you straight to my village. That is where I live. My home is there.

موتی—گھر میں تمہارے ساتھ کون رہتا ہے ؟

Moti—Who lives with you at your home?

جواہر—میرے والد اور والدہ اور میرے ۳ بھائی میرے ساتھ رہتے ہیں -

Jawahir—My father and my mother, and my three brothers live with me at my home.

موتي—تمہارے کے بھائي هيں ؟

Moti—How many brothers have you?

جواهر—میرے ٣ بھائي هيں - دو مجھسے بڑے هيں اور ایک چھوٹا -

Jawahir—I have three brothers. Two of my brothers are older than I and one is younger.

موتی—کیا تمہارا گانو بڑا هے

Moti—Is your village big?

جواهر—نهيں - وہ ایک بالکل چھوٹا سا گانو هے -

Jawahir—No. It is quite a small village.

موتي—تمہارے گانو میں لوگ کیا کرتے هيں ؟

Moti—What do the people in your village do?

جواهر—وے اپني گايوں اور کھيتوں کي دیکھه بھال کرتے هيں - منقریب
وے سب کاشتکار هيں -

Jawahir—They look after their cows and their fields. They are nearly all farmers.

موتي—تمہارے والد کیا کرتے هيں ؟

Moti—What does your father do?

جواهر—میرے والدبھی کاشتکار هيں - انکے کچھه کھیت اور بہت سي
بھینس هيں وہ کھیت جوتتے اور بھینس چراتے هيں - کھیتوں سے همیں گیہوں
ملتا هے - اور بھینسوں سے دودھ -

Jawahir—My father also is a farmer. He has some fields and a good many buffaloes. He ploughs the fields and tends the buffaloes. The fields give us wheat and the buffaloes give us milk.

موتی—گیہوں کو تم کیا کرتے هو ؟

Moti—What do you do with the wheat?

جواہر — کچھہ تو فروخت کر دیتے ہیں اور کچھہ کہاتے ہیں ۔

Jawahir—Some of it we sell and some of it we eat.

موتی — دودہ کا کیا کرتے ہو ؟

Moti—What do you do with the milk ?

جواہر — کچھہ دودہ فروخت کر دیتے ہیں - کچھہ کہاتے ہیں - اور کچھہ کا مکھن اور گھي بناتے ہیں ۔

Jawahir—Some of it we sell, some of it we drink, and some of it we make into ghi and butter.

(2)

اُستاد — اگر تم کسی دوست کو خط لکھنے چاہتے ہو تو کیا کرتے ہو ؟

Teacher—What do you do if you want to send a letter to a friend ?

شاگرد — سب سے پہلے میں جو کچھہ کہنے چاہتا ہوں ایک کاغذ پر لکھتا ہوں ۔

Pupil—First of all I write down on a piece of paper what I want to say.

اُستاد — پھر کیا کرتے ہو ؟

Teacher—What do you do next ?

شاگرد — میں خط کو تہہ کرتا ہوں اور ایک لفافہ میں رکھتا ہوں ۔

Pupil—I fold the letter and put it into an envelope.

اُستاد — بہت ٹھیک ہے - پھر کیا کرتے ہو ؟

Teacher—That is quite true. What do you do next ?

شاگرد — میں لفافہ پر سرنامہ لکھتا ہوں ۔

Pupil—I write the address on the envelope.

اُستاد — سرنامہ کیا ہے ؟

Teacher—What is the address ?

شاگرد—اُس شخص کا نام جسکے پاس خط جارہا ہے اور اُس جگہہ کا نام جہاں وہ رہتا ہے ۔ سرنامہ ہے۔

Pupil—The address is the name of the person to whom the letter is going and the name of place where he lives.

اُستاد—کیا تم لفافہ پر صرف سرنامہ لکھکر ڈاک میں چھوڑ دوگے ؟

Teacher—Will you post the letter simply with the address on the envelope?

شاگرد—نہیں لفافہ پر ایک اسٹامپ لگانا چاهئے ۔

Pupil—No, I must put a stamp on the envelope.

اُستاد—اسٹامپ کہاں ملتا ہے ؟

Teacher—Where do you get the stamp?

شاگرد—میں اسٹامپ ڈاکخانہ سے خرید سکتا ہوں ؟

Pupil—I can buy it at the Post Office.

اُستاد—ایک اسٹامپ کی کیا قیمت ہوتی ہے ؟

Teacher—How much does a stamp cost?

شاگرد—چار پیسے قیمت ہوتی ہے ۔

Pupil—It costs four pice.

اُستاد—چار پیسے میں تم اپنا خط کتنی دور بھیج سکتے ہو ؟

Teacher—How far can you send your letter for four pice?

شاگرد—میں اسے میلوں بلکہ ہزار میل دور تک بھیج سکتا ہوں ۔

Teacher—I can send it any number of miles, even a thousand miles.

اُستاد—کیا کوئی آدمی چار پیسے میں تمہارا خط ایک ہزار میل تک لے جاویگا ؟

Teacher—Will a man carry a letter a thousand miles for you for four pice?

شاگرد—نہیں - ایک میل بھی چار پیسے میں نہ لے جاویگا ۔

Pupil—No, he will not carry it even one mile for four pice.

اُستاد—تب پھر ڈاکخانہ اتنی دور تمہارے خط کو کیسے لے جاتا ھے ؟

Teacher—How does then the post office carry your letter such a long way for four pice?

شاگرد—میں نہیں جانتا ۔

Pupil—I do not know.

اُستاد—میں بتلاتا ھوں کیسے - کیا تم نے کبھی چٹھی رساں کو لیٹر بکس کھولتے ھوئے دیکھا ھے ۔ کتنے خط وہ نکالتا ھے - تمہارا صرف ایک خط انمیں ھے - ھر ایک خط پر چار پیسے والا اسٹمپ چھپا ھے - اتنے چار پیسے ملکر ڈھیر روپیہ ھو جاتا ھے اور وہ سب ڈاکخانہ پاتا ھے ۔

Teacher—I will tell you how. Have you seen a postman opening the letter-box? How many letters he takes out! Your letter is only one among them. Now on every envelope there is a four-pice stamp. So many four-pice make a lot of money and the post office gets all that.

Fables.

(1)

ایک دایہ ایک ضدي لڑکے کو خاموش کرنے کی کوشش کر رھي تھي اور منجملہ دیگر دھمکیوں کے اُسنے لڑکے سے کہا کہ اگر تو رونا بند نہ کریگا تو میں تجھکو بھیڑیئے کے آگے پھینک دونگي - ایک بھیڑیئے نے جو اُسوقت اتفاق سے دروازہ کے باھر گھوم رھا تھا اس بات کو سنا اور یہہ اعتبار کرکے کہ عورت

در حقیقت سچ کہہ رہي هے گهر کے قریب بہت عرصه تک منتظر ٹهہرا رہا ۔ لیکن لڑکا آخرکار شرارت کرتے کرتے تهک گیا اور سو گیا - پس بهیڑیئے کو شام کے ناشته سے مایوس هوکر جنگل کو واپس جانا پڑا - لومڑی راسته میں اُسے ملي اور لاغر اور پریشان دیکهکر پوچهنے لگی که کیا معامله هے که آجکي رات تمهارے هاتهه کچهه نه لگا - اُسنے کہا افسوس میرا حال کچهه نه پوچهو - میں نے بے وقوفي سے دایه کی بات پر اعتبار کیا اور اب مایوس جاتا هوں -

غصه کی حالت کی باتوں پر اعتبار کرنا محض ناداني هے *

A nurse who was endeavouring to quiet a wayward, self-willed child, among other attempts, threatened to throw him out of doors to the Wolf, if he did not leave off crying. A Wolf who chanced to be prowling near the door just at that time, heard the words, and, believing the woman to be in earnest, waited a long while about the house in expectation of seeing her words made good. But at last the child, wearied with its own importunities, fell asleep, and the poor Wolf was forced to return again to the woods without his expected supper. The Fox meeting him, and surprised to see him going home so thin and disconsolate, asked him what the matter was, and how he came to spend no better that night. "Ah, do not ask me," says he; "I was so silly as to believe what the Nurse said, and have been disappointed."

Be not too ready to give credence to the assertions of angry man.

(2)

ایک ضعیف آدمی کے بہت سے لڑکے تھے جو آپس میں اکثر لڑتے رہتے تھے-ضعیف باپ نے بہت سی تدبیریں کیں

لیکن کوئی کار آمد نہ ہوئی-آخرکار اُسنے یہہ حکمت کي - اُس نے حکم دیا کہ میرے سامنے لکڑیونکا ایك گٹھا لاؤ اور لڑکونکو پیش کرو - بعد ازاں اُس نے حکم دیا کہ تم سب یکے بعد دیگرے اپني کل طاقت کے ساتھہ کوشش کرو اور دیکھو کہ تم میں سے کوئي اُسے توڑ سکتا ھے - اُن سبھوں نے کوشش کي لیکن توڑ نہ سکے - چونکہ لکڑي خوب کسی ہوئي بندھی تھی اُسکا توڑنا آدمی کی طاقت سے باھر تھا - بعد ازاں اُس بزرگ نے حکم دیا کہ گٹھا کھول دیا جاوے اور ایك ایك لکڑي اپنے ھر ایك بیٹے کو دیکر فرمایا کہ اب توڑنے کی کوشش کرو - جبکہ ھر ایك نے اُنکو بہ آساني توڑ لیا تو باپ نے انکی طرف مخاطب ہوکر یہہ کہا - اے بیٹو اتفاق کی قوت پر غور کرو - اگر تم اسی طرحسے محبت کے ساتھہ خوب ملکر رھوگے تو کسی انسان کی جرأت نہ ھوگی کہ تمکو نقصان پہونچائے لیکن جب کبھی برادرانہ محبتمیں فرق آئیگا تم بہت جلد تباہ ھوجاؤگے اور ھر ایك دشمن جو تمہارے اوپر حملہ کریگا غالب آئیگا -

نفاق زور کو گھٹا دیتا ھے *

An old man had many sons, who were often falling out with one another. When the old father had exerted his authority and all to no purpose, he at last had recourse to this expedient. He ordered his sons to be called before him, and a short bundle of sticks to be brought, and then commanded them, one by one, to try if, with all their might and strength, could any of them break it. They all tried, but to no purpose, for the sticks being closely and compactly bound up together, it was impossible for the force of man to do it. After this the father ordered the bundle to be untied, and gave a single stick to each of his sons, at the same time bidding him try to break it. Which when each did with all imaginable ease, the father addressed them to this effect:—"O, my sons, behold the power of unity! for if you in like manner would but keep yourselves strictly conjoined in the bonds of friendship it would not be in the power of any mortal to hurt you, but when once the ties of brotherly affection are dissolved, how soon do you fall to pieces and are liable to be violated by every injurious hand that assaults you."

Discord reduceth strength to weakness.

(3)

دو آدمی سڑک پر سفر کررہے تھے - انمیں سے ایک نے ایک کلہاڑی سڑک پر پائی جہانکہ کوئی لکڑی کاٹ رہاتھا - پس اُسنے اسکو اٹھاکر کہا میں نے ایک کلہاڑی پائی ہے - دوسرے نے کہایہہ مت کہو کہ میں نے پائی ہے بلکہ کہو کہ ہم نے پائی ہے کیونکہ ہم دونوں ساتھی ہیں اور ہمکو اسے آپس میں تقسیم کرلینا چاہئیے - لیکن وہ اس پر راضی نہیں ہوتا تھا - خیر وہ بہت دور نہیں پہونچے تھے کہ کلہاڑی کے مالک نے سنکر کہ اسکی کلہاڑی کا کیا ہوا انکا وارنٹ کے ذریعہ سے پیچھا کیا - اسنے جسنے کہ اسکو پایاتھا اپنے ساتھی سے کہا افسوس ہم پکڑگئے - دوسرے نے کہا یہہ مت کہو کہ ہم بلکہ میں پکڑگیا - چونکہ تونے مجھکو مال مفت میں شریک نہیں کیا تھا میں تیرے ساتھہ تکلیف میں بھی شریک نہ ہونگا ·

دوستی قایم رهنے کے واسطے باهمی اتحاد هونا چاهئے *

Two men travelling upon the road, one of them saw an axe lying upon the ground, where somebody had been hewing timber. So taking it up says he, "I have found an axe"—" Do not say I ", says the other, "but we have found ! for, as we are companions, we ought to share it betwixt us." But the first would not consent. However. they had not gone far before the owner of the axe, hearing what became of it pursued them with a warrant, which when the fellow that had it perceived, "Alas!" says he to his companion, "we are undone."—"Nay," says the other, "do not say we, but I am undone; for as you would not let me share the prize, neither will I share the danger with you."

Friendships, to last, should be reciprocal and founded on equality.

مضمون نویسی Essay-writing.

A short literary composition on any subject is called جواب مضمون Essay.

Essays are of three kinds :—

(1) بیانیه یا مشرح Descriptive.

(2) حکایتی Narrative.

(3) مراقبه یا گهرے خیالات ظاهر کرنے والا Reflective,

(1) Description of some thing or place is called the بیانیه یا مشرح مضمون Descriptive Essay.

(2) Narration a historical or supposed event is called حکایتی مضمون Narrative Essay.

(3) Expression of deep thought and the abstract condition as friendship, humility, kindness etc. is called مراقبہ یا گہرے خیالات ظاہر کرنے والا مضمون Reflective Essay.

Examples of Essays.

1. بیانیہ یا مشرح — Descriptive.

جیب گھڑی Watch

جیب گھڑی ایک وقت بتانے والا آلہ ہے - وہ ایک چھوٹی سي چیز ہوتی ہے جو کہ واسکٹ کی جیب میں رکھی جاسکتی ہے - ساعت نما جسپر گھنٹوں کے نشان لگے ہوتے ہیں گھڑی کا چہرہ کہلاتا ہے - اُس پر دو سوئیاں یا کانٹے جڑے رہتے ہیں - ایک چھوٹا اور ایک بڑا - چھوٹا کانٹا گھنٹے دکھاتا ہے اور بڑا منٹ دکھاتا ہے - بہت سی گھڑیوں میں ایک بہت ہی چھوٹی سوئي ہوتی ہے جو پل دکھاتی ہے - گھڑي کے کل پرزے ہمیشہ ایک سونے چاندي یا دیگر کڑے دھات کے خول یا ڈبیا میں جڑے ہوتے ہیں - گھڑی کی کل کا نہایت ضروري پرزہ فولادي کماني ہے - اسی سے گھڑی چلتی ہے - اگر گھڑي کے دونوں جانب ڈھکنے ہوں تو وقت دیکھنے کے لئے ڈھکنوں کو ایک گھنڈي دبا کر کھولنا پڑتا ہے - بعض گھڑیاں زور سے ٹک ٹک کرتي ہیں - بعض میں گھنٹے - آدہ گھنٹے اور پاؤ گھنٹے بھی بجتے ہیں - جب کمانی کھل جاتي ہے تو

کمانی کے لپیٹنو کو چابھی سے کسنا پڑتا ہے ورنہ گھڑی
بند ہو جاتی ہے - بعض اوقات گھڑی کی رفتار دھیمی
ہو جاتی ہے اور وے صحیح وقت نہیں بتلاتیں - گھڑیاں
مختلف قسم اور قد کی ہوتی ہیں - بعض بڑے قد کی
گھڑیاں برجیوں پر لگی ہوتی ہیں - بعض دیوار میں
لٹکائی جاتی ہیں وے دھرم گھڑی کہلاتی ہیں - بعض
میز پر رکھی جاتی ہیں - وے ٹائم پیس کہلاتی ہیں -
آجکل بہت چھوٹی قد کی گھڑیاں جاری ہیں جو کلائی
میں باندھی جاتی ہیں - انکو رست واچ کہتے ہیں -

A watch is a contrivance for showing the time of the day. It is small and can be carried in a waistcoat pocket. The dial on which the hours of the day are marked is called the face of the watch. On it are fitted two pins called 'hands'—one shorter than the other, the shorter one showing the hours and the longer one minutes. Many watches also have a very small needle showing seconds. The machinery of a watch is always fitted into a case which may be made of gold, silver or other hard metal. The most important part of the machinery of a watch is its steel spring, which makes the watch go. If the watch has covers on both sides, the time cannot be seen until the covering over the face is opened by pressing a spring catch. Some watches tick louder than others. Some also sound the hours, half hours, and the quarters. When the spring becomes unwound, the watch has to be wound up to tighten the coils of the spring otherwise it would stop. Sometimes watches go "slow," that is, they do not show the right time but lag behind.

Watches are of various kinds and sizes. Some are of a very large size which are set up on the towers, some are put up on the walls. They are called clocks. Some are kept on tables, and are called time-pieces. Now-a-days watches of very small size are in use which are tied on the wrist, and are called wrist watches.

---

2. حکایت—Narrative.

چمگادڑ اور چرندوں و پرندوں کے درمیان لڑائی

The Bat and the fight between Birds and Beasts.

ایک مرتبہ چرندوں اور پرندوں کے درمیان عرصہ تک لڑائی رہی - کبھی پرند چرندوں پر غالب آتے تھے اور کبھی چرند پرندوں پر - چمگادڑ کبھی چرند ہونے کا دعوی کرتا تھا اور کبھی پرند ہونے کا- کیونکہ وہ ہمیشہ فتح پانے والوں کی جانب رہنے چاهتا تھا - جب وہ اپنے کو چرند ثابت کرنے چاهتا تھا تو چرندوں کے پاس جاتا تھا اور بحث کرتا کہ چونکہ ہمارے دانت ہیں اور اپنے بچوں کو دودھ پلاتے ہیں ہم جانور ہیں - جب وہ چاهتا تھا کہ پرند سمجھا جاوے تو پرندوں کے پاس جاتا اور بحث کرتا کہ جس حال میں اڑ سکتا ہوں میں چرند نہیں ہوں - جب لڑائی جھگڑا رفع دفع ہو گیا چرندوں اور

پرندوں کی بڑی ضیافت ہوئی اور افراط سے کھانے پینے
کا سامان مہیا تھا - جب ضیافت شروع ہوئی چمگادڑ نے
بھی آکر شامل ہونا چاہا - لیکن چرندوں و پرندوں
دونوں نے اسکے چرند یا پرند ہونے کے دعوے کو رد کودیا
اور ضیافت میں سے بھگادیا - چمگادڑ چلا گیا اور مارے
شرم کے ایک سوراخ میں چھپ گیا - تب سے چمگادڑ صرف
اندھیرے میں نکلتے ہیں تاکہ چرند یا پرند اسے دیکھہ
نہ پاویں -

The beasts and birds once had a fight which lasted a long time. Sometimes the birds would get the upperhand, at other times the beasts. The bat claimed to be now a beast and then a bird for it wanted to fight always on the winning side. When it wished to pass off as a beast it would go to the beasts and argue that since it had teeth in its head and gave milk to its young it was a beast. When it wished to be considered a bird it would go to the birds and argue that since it could fly it was not a beast. The quarrel in time was mended and a great feast was given to all the birds and beasts, there being plenty to eat and drink. Just as the feast commenced the bat announced itself and wished to join in, but both birds and beasts refused to claim it as one of them and told it to go away from their feast. The bat, therefore, went away and out of shame hid itself in its hole, and since then bats never come out except when it is dark so that neither birds nor beasts might see them.

3. مراقبه—Reflective.

A

شرافت یا حسن خلق Gentlemanliness.

شرافت اعلی خاندانی اور اصالت کا ثبوت ہے - اشراف آدمی کی ازمایش کئی طرح سے ہو سکتی ہے - دیکھو کہ وہ اپنے نوکر چاکروں پر اپنی طاقت کو کس طرح کام میں لاتا ہے عورتوں اور بچونکا اسکو کیا خیال ہے - اگر وہ افسر ہے تو اپنے ماتحتوں سے کیا سلوک کرتا ہے - اگر مدرس ہے تو اپنے شاگردوں سے کس طرح بولتا ہے - ان حالتوں میں اگر انسان - صبر - اور رحم کے ساتھہ کام کرے تو وہ واقعئی اشراف آدمی ہے اور جو کمزوروں اور مزدوروں کو دکھہ دے وہ نامرد ہے - وہ هرگز طاقتور اور بہادر نہیں - دیو کے برابر طاقت رکھنا بہت اچھی بات ہے لیکن دیو کی طرح اس طاقت کا کام میں لانا خراب ہے - شرافت کے جانچنے کے لئے رحم بہت اچھی اور صحیح جانچ ہے - شریف آدمی اپنا دکھہ سہہ سکتا ہے لیکن اوروں کا دکھہ نہیں دیکھہ سکتا - وہ کبھی اپنی طاقت - دولت - علم اور عیش پر فخر نہیں کرتا - ڈاکٹر فولر نے اشراف آدمی کی بہت اچھی تعریف کی ہے وہ کہتے ہیں کہ جو آدمی برے کاموں سے بچا کاروبار میں سچا - بات کا پکا - نوکروں پر مہربان - مستقل مزاج - محنت کش اور برے کاموں میں همیشہ دلیری نے ساتھہ مستعد و تیار ہو وہ ہی اشراف ہے -

Gentlemanliness is the proof of high birth and nobleness. A gentleman can be tested in several ways.

Notice how he uses his power over his servants. What is his idea towards the females and children. If he is an officer, how he treats his subordinates. If a teacher, how he speaks to his pupils. In such positions if a man acts with wisdom, patience and mercy he is really a gentleman but the one who oppresses the labourers and the weak is not a man. He is not strong and brave. It is good to have strength like a giant but to use that strength like a giant is bad. To test the gentlemanliness mercy is the better and right test. A gentleman can tolerate his pains but cannot see the pains of others. He is never proud of his power, wealth, knowledge and comforts.

Dr. Fuller has praised highly a gentleman.—The man who keeps himself from the evil deeds, is honest in his dealings, is abiding by his words, is kind to the servants, is persevering, is laborious and always prepared boldly for great deeds is a gentleman.

B

دینا Give

دینا لینے سے مبارک ہے - اپنے دل کے سب سے اچھے خزا نے دے ڈالو - خوشنما کائنات سے دینا سیکھو - دیکھو دریا بہکر سمندر میں گرتے ہیں اور اپنا سارا خزانہ فیاضي اور وفور کے ساتھہ اُنڈیل دیتے ہیں - تاہم دینے میں اُنکي مدد کرنے کے لئے چھپے ہوے سوتے نکلتے ہیں یا اگر ضرورت ہوتي تو آسمان سے بارش اُنکی پرورش کرتي ہے - عظیم الشان پھولونکو دیکھو اپني پر تکلف خوشبو پھیلاتے ہیں - ہوا کو خوشبو سے جو اُنکی خوبصورتی سے نکلتي

ے بھر دیتے ھیں - تاھم اُنکے افراط سے خرچ کردینے سے کوئی کمی نہیں ھوتی انکی مادر زمین اُنکو پھر تازہ زندگی سے معمور کردیتی ھے - اسی طرح اپنی محبت دو (یعنی محبت کرو) اور مانگو مت (یعنی یہہ نہ چاھو کہ دوسرا بھی تم سے محبت کرے) - اور عوض کا انتظار نہ کرو اور جتنا زیادہ تم اپنے چھوتے سے ذخیرہ سے خرچ کروگے خدا تمکو دوگنا فیاضی کے ساتھہ اور زیادہ دیگا -

خدا اُن کو زیادہ پر زیادہ دیتا ہے جو اوروں کی مدد کرنے کو تیار رھتے ھیں -

It is more blessed to give than to receive. Learn to give from the fair Nature. Give your heart's best treasures. Lo! the rivers flow on and eventually fall into the sea. Despite this more fountains spring forth to help them in flowing. If there need be rain from heaven brings them up. See the magnificent flowers which spread their odour too unsparingly and fill the air with the scent emanating from their beauty. Despite it no shortage is produced by their giving lavishly. This mother earth renews with fresh life. Precisely in the same way love *i. e.* give love and not expect its return. Have love for all and do not expect others to do the same to you. Don't wait for the exchange for your good. The more you will spendout of your reservoir the more abundantly with double generosity will God give you.

God gives more and more to those who are ready to help others.

خطوط نویسی وغیرہ Letter-writing etc.

The writer of a letter is called کاتب 'kátib' and to whom a letter is written is called مکتوب الیہ 'maktúb aleh.'

When writing letters it is essential to keep in mind the rank and position of the person whom it is addressed to *i. e.* whether the person addressed is Senior or Junior or Equal.

Some Forms of Address.

القاب و آداب

Elders or Seniors.

والد Father—جناب قبلہ کونین دام ظلکم العالی—
بعد ادائے اداب و تسلیمات عرض پرداز ہوں کہ......وغیرہ

دادا Grandfather—قبلہ دو جہاں مخدوم مخدومان
دامت اقبالہ—بعد تمنائے قدمبوسی عرض ہے کہ.....وغیرہ

ماموں Uncle—جناب ماموں صاحب قبلہ کونین و
کعبہ دارین سلامت—بعد ادائے آداب و تسلیمات فدویانہ
کے عرض ہے کہ........وغیرہ

Juniors.

بیٹا Son—

(۱) عزیز ازجان سلمہ اللہ الرحمٰن—دعا - آں عزیز
کا خط ملا......وغیرہ

(۲) برخوردار سعادت اطوار - دعاے ترقی علم و اقبال ......وغیرہ

چھوٹا بھائی Younger brother—

(۱) برادر عزیز سلمہ اللہ تعلےٰ—دعا.........وغیرہ

(۲) برادر عزیزالقدر عزیز از جان سلمہ.....وغیرہ

بھتیجا Nephew—عزیزی سلمہ—دعا - مسرت نامہ ملا - حالات سے اگاھی ہوئی.........وغیرہ

چھوٹی بہن Sister—ھمشیرہ عزیزہ سلمہا—دعاے ترقی عمر کے بعد واضع ھو.........وغیرہ

Equals.

دوست Friend—

(۱) مخلص بےریا زاد محبتہ—تسلیم - آپ کی علالت کا حال معلوم ھوا......وغیرہ

(۲) شفیقی زاد محبتہ—اداب عرض - محبت نامہ ملا......وغیرہ

بیوی Wife—

(۱) مونث تنہائی من -

(۲) عفت پناہ عصمت ماب -

(۳) ھم دم و ھمراز من سلامت—بعد سلام وشوق ملاقات کے معلوم ھو.........وغیرہ

Letter to Father.

خط والد کے نام

جناب قبلہ کونین و کعبہ دارین دام ظلکم العالی - بعد ادائے آداب وتسلیمات عرض پرداز ہوں کہ میں حضور والا سے رخصت ہو کر بفضل اللہ تعالے آگرہ پہونچ گیا - جناب منصف صاحب کا سفارش نامہ ہیڈ ماسٹر صاحب کی خدمت میں پیش کیا - جناب ممدوح نے مولوی امام الدین صاحب کو بلا کر مجھے انکے سپرد کر دیا - مولوی صاحب موصوف بہت ہی خوش خلق و نیک بخت ہیں - فوراً میرے لئے انتظام کر دیا اور میں بورڈنگ ہاوس میں داخل ہو گیا - مجھے یہاں کسی قسم کی تکلیف نہیں ہے - مجھے یقین ہے کہ میں یہاں فضل خدا سے اور حضور کی دعا سے نہایت کامیاب رہونگا - جناب والدہ ماجدہ صاحبہ کی خدمت میں اداب عرض عزیزان برادر و ہمشیرہ کو بہت بہت دعا -

خادم ——

Letter to Son.

خط بیٹے کے نام

از کلکتہ ۱۲ جولائی ۱۹۳۵ ع

عزیز از جان سلمہ اللہ الرحمٰن دعا اں عزیز کا خط ملا - تم نے جو چند اشیائے ضروری کی خریداری کے لئے

خرچ طلب کیا ہے اسکو میں بخوشی روانہ کرتا ہوں - مبلغ ۱۰ روپیہ کا منی آرڈر دو چار روز میں تمکو ملجاویگا - خیال رہے کہ فیشن وغیرہ میں خرچ کرنا محض بد وضعی وفضول خرچی ہے- ہر طالب علم کو بہر حال اس سے اجتناب چاہئے -تمہارے چھوٹے بھائی اور بہن تسلیم عرض کرتے ہیں اور تمہاري والدہ دعا کرتی ہیں -

راقم الدعا——

Letter to Friend.

خط دوست کے نام

کرم فرمائے من جناب لچھمن سنگھہ صاحب زاد عنایتہ——بعد آداب کے عرض پرداز ہوں کہ محبت نامہ آپکا وصول ہوا - آپ میري عدم موجودگی میں تشریف لائے اور میں اتفاق سے باہر چلا گیا تھا • بہت افسوس رہا - شادي کے واسطے گاڑی دینے میں مجھے کیا آپ سے عذر ہو سکتا ہے- ہمارے آپکے مراسم پشت ہا پشت سے چلے آتے ہیں - آپ کی عزت ہماري عزت ہے - اگر ایسی چیزیں درکار ہوں جو مکان پر موجود نہ ہوں تو وہ کہیں نہ کہیں سے مہیا کر سکتا ہوں - اور اپنا فرض تصور کرتا ہوں -

زیادہ نیاز

رام سینگھہ

RECEIPT

رسید

منکہ موہن لال ساکن فیض‌آباد کا ہوں جو کہ منمقر نے دو سو روپیہ بابت قیمت اینٹ مسٹر پ ل صاحب بہادر افسر میونسپلٹی فیض‌آباد سے وصول پائے لہذا یہہ چند کلمے بطریق رسید لکھدیئے کہ سند رہے اور ضرورت کے وقت کام آے فقط -

۱۰ جنوری ۱۹۳۸ ع

PRONOTE.

رقعہ عند الطلب

منکہ رگھبر دیال ولد رام دیال قوم کایستھہ ساکن محلہ گاڑي پورہ قصبہ رام پور ضلع مرادآباد کاہوں منمقر نے مبلغ پانسو روپیہ کہ جسکے نصف دو سو پچاس روپیہ ہوتے ہیں - بدست لالہ رام سہاے ولد گنگا سہاے قوم کایستھہ ساکن محلہ کٹرہ شہر مرادآباد بحساب دو روپیہ سیکڑہ سود ماہواري مقام کٹرہ شہر مرادآباد لیا اسکو ادا و بےباق کرونگا - لہذا یہہ چند کلمے بطور رقعہ عندالطلب کے لکھہ دیئے تاکہ سند رہے اور وقت پر کام آے -

المرقوم ۳ مارچ ۱۹۳۶ ع

PETITION TO HEADMASTER FROM A STUDENT.

عرضی بنام ہیڈ ماسٹر

بحضور جناب ہیڈ ماسٹر صاحب گورنمنٹ ہائی اسکول پرتاب گڑہ دام اقبالہ -

جناب عالی -

بکمال اداب گذارش ہے کہ فدوی کل سے تپ لرزہ کے باعث مجبور ہو کر مدرسہ سے غیر حاضر ہے - علاج ڈاکٹری کررہا ہوں امید ہے جلد صحت حاصل ہو جاویگی - فدوی عرض پرداز ہے کہ تاوقت صحت یابی غیر حاضری میری معاف فرمائی جاوے -

عرضی

فدوی گیان چند طالبعلم درجہ ششم

مورخہ ۲۱ فروری ۱۹۳۵ ع

[THE END]